StyleCity
PARIS

StyleCity
PARIS

With over 400 colour photographs and 6 maps

 Thames & Hudson

with Salad a

- Beef
- Salmon (

9,15

Nos Carpac

,00€

7,5

Contents

Street Wise

Style Traveller

Series concept and editor: Lucas Dietrich
Texts: Phyllis Richardson
Restaurant consultant and texts: Sébastien Demorand
Original design and map concept: The Senate
Jacket and book design: Grade Design Consultants
Maps: Peter Bull

Specially commissioned photography by
Ingrid Rasmussen and Anthony Webb

Although every effort has been made to ensure that
the information in this book is as up-to-date and as
accurate as possible at the time of going to press,
some details are liable to change.

First published in the United Kingdom in 2003 by
Thames & Hudson Ltd, 181A High Holborn,
London WC1V 7QX

www.thamesandhudson.com

© 2003 Thames & Hudson Ltd, London
Reprinted, with corrections, 2003

British Library Cataloguing-in-Publication Data
A catalogue record for this book is available from the
British Library
ISBN 0-500-21006-3

Printed in China by C & C Offset Printing Co Ltd

How to Use This Guide

The book features two principal sections: **Street Wise** and **Style Traveller**.

Street Wise, which is arranged by neighbourhood, features areas that can be covered in a day (and night) on foot and includes a variety of locations – cafés, shops, restaurants, museums, performance spaces, bars – that capture local flavour or are lesser-known destinations.

The establishments in the **Style Traveller** section represent the city's best and most characteristic locations – 'worth a detour' – and feature hotels (**sleep**), restaurants (**eat**), cafés and bars (**drink**), boutiques and shops (**shop**) and getaways (**retreat**).

Each location is shown as a circled number on the relevant neighbourhood map, which is intended to provide a rough idea of location and proximity to major sights and landmarks rather than precise position. Locations in each neighbourhood are presented sequentially by map number. Each entry in the **Style Traveller** has two numbers: the top one refers to the page number of the neighbourhood map on which it appears; the second number is its location.

For example, the visitor might begin by selecting a hotel from the **Style Traveller** section. Upon arrival, **Street Wise** might lead him to the best joint for coffee before guiding him to a house-museum nearby. After lunch he might go to find a special jewelry store listed in the **shop** section. For a memorable dining experience, he might consult his neighbourhood section to find the nearest restaurant crossreferenced to **eat** in **Style Traveller**.

Street addresses are given in each entry, and complete information – including email and web addresses – is listed in the alphabetical **contact** section. Travel and contact details for the destinations in **retreat** are given at the end of **contact**.

Legend

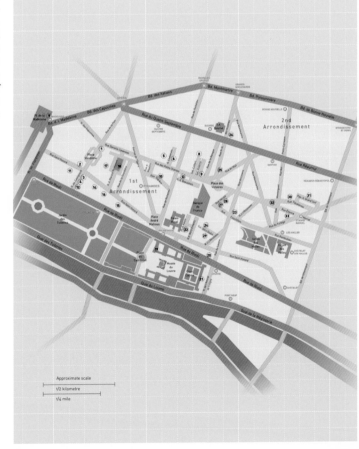

②	Location
▮	Museums, sights
▮	Gardens, squares
Ⓜ	Métro stops
▬	Principal street
▨	Secondary road

Approximate scale
1/2 kilometre
1/4 mile

PARIS

In the hearts and imaginations of people around the world, Paris, of all the great cities, hardly needs introduction. Even in those of us who have yet to set foot in the City of Lights, it is remembered as a beacon of artistic and literary endeavour after the war, a place where creativity and philosophy emanated from the cafés of the Left Bank like so much Gitanes cigarette smoke. 'Like Paris in the twenties', people say of any city drawing an international bohemian crowd with high culture on the cheap and high-intensity living to match. And no other city quite captures the particular 'romance' of Paris. This ineluctable appellation has perhaps become cliché, overused, commercialized, trivialized, but the real thing is still there for the savvy visitor.

Like any ancient city, modern Paris is built on many layers and exists on many levels of perception, physical, historical, emotional. One reason that Paris retains its aura is, of course, its survival – more or less intact – through the great wars. Coveted by invaders who would rather own it than destroy it, it is a city marked by large personalities and grandiose expressions: from King Philippe-Auguste, who chartered the first University in the thirteenth century, and the spendthrift François I, who rebuilt the Louvre in Italian Renaissance style and promoted humanism, to the even more ostentatious Sun King, who left the Louvre in favour of Versailles, and Napoleon, who added his own imperial monuments, the Arc de Triomphe, the Arc du Carrousel, the column of the place Vendôme. It was his nephew Napoleon III, who left probably the most visible urban legacy through the work of his urban engineer Georges (later, Baron) Haussmann. Haussmann 'modernized' Paris – clearing away vast areas of medieval buildings (which urban historians decry to this day) to make way for the grand boulevards that give Paris so much of its opulent character – as well as building schools, churches and synagogues.

Modern democratic and coalition rulers were understandably more restrained than their autocratic predecessors, but still the city has been touched by great architectural vision even in the late-twentieth century: Georges Pompidou's sponsorship of the ground-breaking 'high-tech' art centre designed by Richard Rogers and Renzo Piano in 1977 and Valéry Giscard d'Estaing's support for the audacious conversion of the Gare d'Orsay railway station into a celebration of art. In the 1980s and 1990s, Mitterand's controversial *grands projets* (the Bastille Opera House, the Grand Louvre project, the new library, the Grande Arche de la Défense) and most recently, the creation of large, meticulously landscaped parks just on the perimeter of the centre – André Citroën (p. 36) and Bercy (p. 100) – confirm a forward-looking determination to ensure that Paris continues to embrace bold modernity and urban innovation.

Such ambitious projects remind us that, though so much of the past has been preserved here, this is a cosmopolitan city at the forefront of fashion, design and the arts. Paris is where artists, musicians, writers flock to be inspired, to be with other creative minds like themselves. Why? Is the love of beauty and style particularly French? Is the sense of romance engendered by past struggles, by strong traditions of language and culture? Almost as well known for the outspokenness of its citizenry as for its unparalleled sense of style, Paris's streets have been the scene of the world's most famous revolution, of popular protests, foreign occupation and liberation, unbridled celebration, and they continue to be a public staging ground.

What visitors will find in Paris today is a city bursting with creative energy, not in the edgy, street-conscious way of, say, London, but in a manner reflecting a more artisanal – and at times flamboyant – attitude to creativity. The most talked-about hotels are lavishly decorated in the spirit of the Empire or in a particularly French brand of minimalism; the best restaurants combine the talents of the most innovative designers with young chefs trained in the tradition-al French methods but willing to experiment with global cuisines. The grand old fashion houses are still lined up around the Faubourg St Honoré and the Champs-Élysées, but so are the new names, and in pockets around the Marais, the Bastille and Montmartre, young designers with backroom ateliers are producing clothing, objects and furniture that one day may be the next big thing but for now are wonderfully unique creations you won't see anywhere else. The late-night club scene still thrives, reinvented, revitalizing the old cabarets of Montmartre and in the once-disused spaces around the Bastille and the République. Creative hopefuls have also flowed into and reinvigorated outer 'villages', such as Canal St-Martin and Belleville. Café culture through-out the capital is alive and well, with many an established and revamped *terrasse* filled with ani-mated conversationalists or lone drinkers immersed in *Le Monde* or watching the world go by.

Paris, as writer Edmund White contends, is truly the city of the flâneur, where an aim-less wander can bring unexpected rewards around every corner – the glimpse of a medieval square, an exquisite boutique, an enticing café or one of those grand architectural gestures in which Paris's place in history and the imagination is writ large.

Street Wise

Latin Quarter • St-Germain-des-Prés • Montparnasse •
Rue du Bac • Chaillot • Champs-Élysées • Right Bank •
Palais-Royal • Montorgueil • Grands Boulevards • Pigalle •
Montmartre • Beaubourg • Marais • Canal St-Martin • Bercy •

Latin Quarter
St-Germain-des-Prés
Montparnasse

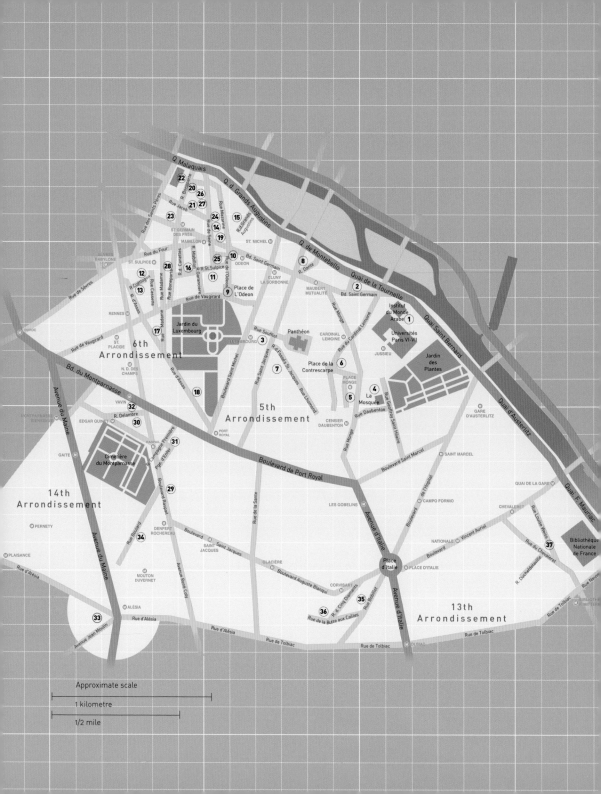

The Latin Quarter is where Paris's first university was founded in the 12th century. Latin was the language of learning, and so gave its name to an area focused on enlightenment. The area today, bordered roughly by the contrasting but equally wonderful Jardin du Luxembourg and Jardin des Plantes, is still one of multi-cultural influences, of students and new bohemians. A lot of those students and travellers congregate around the boulevard St Michel, where cheap cafés and fast-food restaurants outnumber independent traders. This is a vibrant, but often overbusy, neighbourhood, pulsing with the energy and excitement of youth. It is fitting that two of Paris's most significant Islamic institutions should be near this historic seat of learning. The Mosquée, built in the 1920s, was erected as a tribute to North African efforts in the First World War. Its exquisite decor is the work of a multitude of North African craftsmen. A small tea salon brings a refreshing exoticism to the quarter. Farther north, on a picturesque quaiside setting adjacent to the large modern university complex, the Institut du Monde Arabe shows the modern face of Islamic-French architecture with a technologically advanced design by Jean Nouvel. As a centre for art and culture it exudes all the excitement of dedication and learning that has distinguished the quarter for centuries.

Another influential educational centre is several blocks west in St-Germain-des-Prés. The Ecole des Beaux Arts is a world-renowned institution that infuses the entire neighbourhood with artistic aspirations, which, in turn, radiate throughout Paris and beyond. Now that its postwar literary associations have been overtaken by its modern design and art connections, the quarter is known for furnishings, decorative objects and art from the early to mid-20th century. In addition to being a home to the galleries, St-Germain-des-Prés has a reputation for its fine shopping district, filled with smart, artistically inclined boutiques, not the emerging talents found in Montmartre or even in parts of the Marais, but designers who have managed to achieve enough high-profile success to maintain a shop in this glittering neighbourhood.

Before you wander from the delights of St-Germain-des-Prés to the even more upmarket offerings of the Rue du Bac, we suggest dipping south to the villagey streets of the Butte-aux-Cailles, especially around the rue des Cinq-Diamants, and Montparnasse, long known as a bohemian enclave. Here are the less glamorous but equally important parts, picturesque old neighbourhoods with restaurants, cafés and streets that, being just outside the limelight, gain in character what they lose in urban frenzy.

1 ## Institut du Monde Arabe
1, rue des Fossés-St-Bernard

The centre for Arabic arts and culture was designed by French architect Jean Nouvel in 1987 around the concept of a *moucharabieh* but used in a distinctly modern way with photo-electric cells in the exterior cladding that adjust the amount of light entering the building to protect the museum pieces inside. There have been problems with some of the more technical aspects of the design – the cells don't always function perfectly – but the building itself is still a graceful piece of architecture with Islamic elements and patterns woven into the modern white façade and the added appeal of the white-paved square spreading out to the road. Apart from the permanent collection of art, artifacts and decorative objects, the institute hosts temporary exhibitions, films and lectures on art, architecture, literature and history. The stylishly modern café Loubnane serves sandwiches and drinks.

FRESH BEGINNINGS

2 ## Le Petit Pontoise
9, rue de Pontoise

Last time we walked into this lovely bistro, we encountered a dozen baskets of fresh wild mushrooms (boletus, chanterelle), others filled with sublimely red raspberries and dark blackberries; on another table were arranged *potimarrons* (small pumpkins with a chestnut flavour), Espelette pepper braids from the Pays Basque and two kilos of fresh walnuts. On a wall, a small sign reads, 'We'll start cooking once you've ordered. Please be patient.' If only such freshness of ingredients and scrupulousness could spread to every single bistro in the city. Try the plain and simple roasted chicken with purée; you'll never eat it anywhere else.

SIMPLE AND HEARTY

3 ## Les Fontaines
9, rue Soufflot

It doesn't look promising: just an average neighbourhood brasserie, quite old-fashioned. The décor is forgettable, unless you want to experience a mid-1970s atmosphere. But this isn't important to the huge crowd of diners, only too happy to sit shoulder to shoulder on one of the narrow benches, ordering pâtés, thick ribsteaks with great pommes soufflées (potato puffs), milk-fed lamb, game (from October to late January) and tarte Tatin. Who would want a place like this to change?

HAMMAM AND MINT TEA

4   La Mosquée de Paris

150

TEA CEREMONIES

5   La Maison des Trois Thés

150

SECRET GARDEN

6   Hôtel des Grandes Ecoles

120

TOUT LE JOUR

7   Café de la Nouvelle Mairie

19–21, rue des Fossés-St-Jacques

This is the kind of place you can visit at any time of day: a cup of coffee and the newspapers around 9 am, a quick bite at lunchtime, a beer at 4 pm, an apéritif with friends around 7. A dream of a bistro, with its terrace facing a lovely little square, its green benches inside, its jazzy background music, not to mention a short but clever wine list (try a Morgon from the Beaujolais region or a Coteaux du Languedoc) and an irreproachable cuisine, essentially based on charcuterie or farm cheese plates and a plat du jour.

GOURMET COOKBOOKS

8   Librairie Gourmande

4, rue Dante

In the city long thought to be the world's culinary capital, it makes sense to have a look at what they consider a good cookbook. The problem at the Librairie Gourmande is that there are so many and not just the latest titles. There are old editions of some American and British cookbooks as well as the full stock of French titles. The small, cramped space and tables outside are brimming with old traditional and modern fusion recipes. From Escoffier to Pierre Hermé to Jamie Oliver.

BUILDINGS BY THE BOOK

9   Librairie le Moniteur

7, place de l'Odéon

In its spacious modern premises on the Place de l'Odéon, le Moniteur offers books on architecture, design and building, as well as sponsoring a number of its own publications – books, pamphlets, CD-ROMs – having started with the magazine *Moniteur des travaux publics* in 1903. Today the Paris bookshop is an invaluable source for architecture, design and building enthusiasts.

SCULPTURE IN METALS AND GEMS
10 Galerie Hélène Porée
1, rue de l'Odéon

As you might expect from a jewelry shop that is called a gallery, there are pieces here that you could frame and hang on the wall, architectural pieces, pieces in trompe l'oeil that are cleverly faceted to appear more three-dimensional than they are, and pieces that are like jewel-topped sculpture. What you might not expect is that there are pieces that are very reasonably priced. The clear, elegant space is lined with cabinets full of necklaces, earrings and rings by Alexandra Bahlmann, Cathy Chotard, Anuschka Wald and Escher-like pieces by Claude and Françoise Chavent. An upstairs room is used for exhibitions.

SOPHISTICATED FOLK
11 Vanessa Bruno
25, rue St-Sulpice

Vanessa Bruno's clothes have something of a 1970s gypsy look about them, but with definite contemporary style. Blouses with lacey bodices, high necks and gathered sleeves are paired with bias-cut cardigans and flounce skirts. There is a range of chunky leather boots and bags, as well as more streamlined footwear, all with a relaxed attitude that's more folk than fashion. A pale yellow needlecord trouser suit with black floral print is hard to resist. This, her first shop, has homey rough wood floors, but also a cut-out purple wall and funky ornamental chandelier to signal an all-over sense of design. Her new shop on the pricey rue de Castiglione goes modern with glossy white-enamel fixtures contrasting with the fresco-style wall treatments.

PATCHWORK PRINCE
12 Daniel Jasiak
174

SKIN DEEP
13 Peggy Huyn Kinh
171

TO DRINK LIKE A …
14 Fish/La Boissonnerie
69, rue de Seine

If you've already been to Paris with a hip travel guide in your pocket, you might have run into this wine bar owned by a young American named Juan Sanchez (ask for the address of his wine shop), who knows French vineyards better than most French. Each week he changes the ten wines served by the glass, a clever means to ensure oenophiles return. His viticultural coups de cœur often take him to the Rhône valley, the Languedoc-Roussillon or the Riviera (check the fantastic Côtes de Provence Château de Roquefort, for instance). And to fill stomachs, the food is just right, mainly based on pasta and vegetables.

RAW ARTISTRY
15 Ze Kitchen Galerie
144

JUST PLAIN GOOD
16 Les Charpentiers
10, rue Mabillon

One sometimes wonders why the city doesn't have more places like Les Charpentiers ('the carpenters'): a pleasant, old-fashioned décor, friendly waiters, affordable wines, customers from around the corner or from around the globe, and simple classic French food, quite well done: try some charcuteries, a tomato salad (with great olive oil, parsley and young white onions) or a blanquette 'Marie Louise', with its pieces of veal swimming in a generous creamy sauce, garnished with dots of carrots and button onions. Paris should always taste like this.

THE WELL-DRESSED CHILD
17 Oona L'Ourse
72, rue Madame

Jeanne Fichard's bestselling line of high-quality children's clothing does not look set to diminish even as economies fluctuate; they're just too beautifully designed and detailed. Naturally hued sweaters, dresses, trousers, coats, blouses in soft linen, lambswool and cashmere might seem too precious to risk growing out of but her many fans, big and small, don't appear to mind the mini extravagance.

A NEW MODERN
18 Le Café des Délices
146

ARCHITECT-DESIGNED FURNITURE
19 Galerie 54
54, rue Mazarine

This is an area filled with galleries of every type but all are generally of a high quality, so collections need to be distinctive. Though this isn't the only gallery dealing in modern French design, it is one that does its job well. Eric Touamleaume and Jean-Pierre Bouchard specialize in 'furniture made by architects and in elements of architecture'. Charlotte Perriand, Jean Prouvé, Le Corbusier and Pierre Jeanneret are the focus of their collection, along with Serge Mouille, Georges Jouve and Alexandre Noll.

THE QUINTESSENCE OF ROMANCE
20 L'Hôtel

126

IN BLACK AND WHITE
21 IF
20, rue Jacob

Their aim is to offer day-to-day items that are simple but beautiful and 'free of superficial pretension'. Originally established in Taiwan, IF slipped quietly but nobly into the St-Germain-des-Prés shopping district with a shop stocked full of items in black or white against a similar backdrop designed by the doyenne of French minimalism, Andrée Putman (see also p. 124). Their selection is eclectic, including everything from a range of black knitwear by Iro Iwata (made in France) to glassware, ceramics and tableware in soft, basic forms. There are also throws, cushions and lightly scented candles, all with a sense of quiet luxury about them.

20TH-CENTURY FRENCH CLASSICS
22 Galerie Yves Gastou

162

23 La Hune

170, boulevard St-Germain

A famed bookstore with notoriously late opening hours, La Hune is a white hub of culture on the *grand boulevard*. La Hune is known for its art and design books, and its wide glass windows and white interior with discreet designerly elements that demonstrate an architectural awareness. Books on art, style, architecture and graphics are carefully arranged on the galleried mezzanine level overlooking the street, while a good range of fiction (in French) is on the ground floor. A number of the titles upstairs are in English and quite a few are laid out on the counters under the windows, where you can browse and throw the occasional glance at the street scene below. Those suffering from vertigo might be wary of the slightly disconcerting angle of the stairs.

CAFÉ OF THE ARTS

24 La Palette

43, rue de Seine

As the name suggests, La Palette is a café with genuine artistic leanings. Its proximity to the École des Beaux Arts and setting in an area filled with galleries mean that it draws clientele from both. Large, colourful oil paintings and exhibition posters contribute to the arty Parisian stereotype. This is a traditional French café with all the classic offerings, occasionally brusque waiters and fine corner spot for outdoor tables. The daily specials are fresh, well-prepared and worth trying, even if you don't completely understand the description.

FLORAL SENSATIONS

25 Christian Tortu

167

MODERN FRENCH AND NEW-DESIGN FURNITURE

26 Alexandre Biaggi

DESIGNED AFTER A FASHION

27 Lagerfeld Gallery

40, rue de Seine

Not so much a gallery as a place for the slow, boutique style of shopping that's become popular with designers of late, though the title is appropriate enough in a neighbourhood filled with art and antiques showrooms. Lagerfeld Gallery is actually the name of the particular line of prêt à porter that is showcased in this shop decorated in Andrée Putman's (see also p. 124) signature luxurious minimalism – dark wood, rich-coloured fabrics all streamlined against pure white. This isn't all about the clothes, as the design objects, books and black-and-white photographs of buildings by Tadao Ando will make clear. There is even a room at the back to sit and read the latest fashion magazines between couture decisions or while you wait for that Lagerfeld fan to emerge from the changing room.

SWEET ARTS

28 Pierre Hermé

PATRONS OF CONTEMPORARY ART

29 Fondation Cartier

261, boulevard Raspail

Architect Jean Nouvel (see also the Institut du Monde Arabe, p. 17) has once again created a stand-out structure for a cultural centre. This time it is the Fondation Cartier pour l'art contemporain, an organization created according to the vision of Alain Dominique Perrin, president of Cartier International, in 1984. In 1994 the programme of corporate-sponsored arts moved into Nouvel's space of shifting glass panes, providing glimpses of the vibrant art scene inside. With the stated aim of 'building up a collection of work by living artists that is a reflection of the age', the foundation buys, commissions and exhibits, as well as staging theatre, music and dance performances. Artworks date from the 1980s with French artists such as Arman César, Raymond Hains and Jean-Pierre Raynaud representing the commitment to national creativity, while an array of such international figures as Sam Francis, Joan Mitchell and James Turrell demonstrate Cartier's global mission 'to place modern art at the heart of the preoccupations of the modern world'.

JAZZY CAFÉ

30 Rosebud

11 bis, rue Delambre

A 1950s-style jazzy venue that attracts a crowd of 30- to 50-somethings who come to drink cocktails and relive a certain dusky retro glamour. The barmen in formal white jackets purportedly serve the best Bloody Mary in Paris. The ambience has an American vibe, though there are plenty of locals to keep the dress style elevated. Come in for refreshment after a visit to the Fondation Cartier or cap your dinner at Le Dôme with an atmospheric postprandial drink.

STREET OF LOCAL COLOUR

31 Passage d'Enfer

Off boulevard Raspail

This is not a tourist destination, it doesn't even have any shops or cafés, but if you happen to be in the neighbourhood, on your way to the Cimetière Montparnasse, the Fondation Cartier (previous column) or Le Vin des Rues (p. 26), then the small detour along this cobblestoned lane might just provide the extra bit of atmosphere to put you in the Paris neighbourhood mood. The delightful, somewhat concealed enclave of uninterrupted terraces of houses with shutters painted in different pastel shades is one of the area's best-kept secrets.

ART DÉCO AND SEAFOOD

32 Le Dôme

108, boulevard du Montparnasse

Some believe this is where you'll find Paris's best sole meunière. This 1930s brasserie is truly a top choice for upper-class fish and shellfish dishes. And there's the place itself: a breathtakingly beautiful Art Déco interior with velvet benches, black-and-white photos on the walls, plaques commemorating some famous patrons (do you want to sit where Picasso sat, or perhaps Apollinaire?) and tuxedoed waiters moving silently from table to table. What to eat? Try the *mouclade* (mussels in a fantastic creamy curry sauce), the fried baby squid, the sole (the fish is presented whole so the waiter can fillet it in front of you) or any kind of shellfish platter. Expensive, unforgettable.

SEASONAL PLEASURES

33 La Régalade

34 Le Vin des Rues
21, rue Boulard

This tiny bistro was photographer Robert Doisneau's favourite. What more to say? That it still looks as it did back in the 1950s, with the owner behind the zinc counter, the napkin rack with the names of the regulars, the dozens of Beaujolais bottles stacked here and there... There used to be a table d'hôte in the kitchen, but sadly patrons cannot sit there any more. The food reflects the timeless atmosphere: lentil and lardon salad, great sausages from Lyon, veal rib. If the weather's sunny, why not find a table outside for a relaxed apéritif of white wine?

LINING UP IN THE BUTTE-AUX-CAILLES
35 L'Avant-Goût
26, rue Bobillot

For great contemporary French cooking at reasonable prices (though the price of the prix fixe menu nudges gently upwards, it remains one of the city's best bargains), it's worth seeking out this tiny, warm bistro near the Butte aux Cailles. There's no point in showing up without a booking, unless you're willing to start queuing outside two hours ahead of time for lunch or even longer for dinner. The place is always crowded, for everybody knows that chef Christophe Beaufront's market-bistro cuisine is both artful (the spicy *pot au feu* is the classic) and tasty and that the welcome is always excellent.

NEIGHBOURHOOD NIGHTS
36 Rue de la Butte-aux-Cailles
Rue des Cinq-Diamants
Off rue Bobillot

- La Folie en Tête, 33, rue de la Butte-aux-Cailles
- Chez Paul, 22, rue de la Butte-aux-Cailles
- Les Cailloux, 58, rue des Cinq-Diamants

Just south of the Place d'Italie a confluence of pedestrianized streets shows a different side of Paris, the charming village full of lovely squares, small cafés and ethnic restaurants, students and local residents young and old. The atmosphere is much more casual and relaxed than the smarter and more touristy areas, and yet there is something to discover here in a pleasant, quiet and characterful setting. Le Petite Alsace is a private street but you can still have a polite look at the group of regional-style country houses. Not so quiet, however, is La Folie en Tête, which is a popular bar but also a lively night spot, particularly popular with students. It serves a renowned

and flavourful 'ti punch' (which reputedly packs one), as well as wine, Belgian beers and the ever-popular cloudy comfort of *pastis*. There's live music or a DJ on Saturdays and the place is open until 2 am. You might try dinner at Chez Paul, an old-fashioned restaurant with the feel of an old photograph, although it's a bit more modern than it looks. It's worth a try for age-old earthy classics like marrowbones, oxtail terrine, a great *pot au feu* (cheap but perfect beef cuts in a dense bouillon), milk-fed piglet roasted with sage and the always delicious rum baba. Accompany these with a bottle of Mâcon or Chablis and seize the day – or night. Those seeking a modern, Italian-influenced cuisine with an intelligent wine list popular with Parisians should head to the recently opened Les Cailloux, where the two rues meet.

CUTTING-EDGE ART GALLERIES
37 Rue Louise-Weiss
Off boulevard Vincent Auriol

Very near the Chevaleret Métro stop, this seemingly unprepossessing street behind the Bibliothèque National is a mecca for contemporary art and design. Together with rue Duchefdelaville and rue du Chevaleret, it has become part of a new artistic quarter in Paris, showing its best face in monthly art fairs in which the galleries take part in joint public exhibitions. The galleries range from the modern-baroque Galerie Praz-Delavallade to the ultra-minimalist Galerie Kreo featuring designs by the hot Parisian duo Ronan and Erwan Bouroullec (see also p. 174). These are not the kinds of galleries you'll find around the Beaux Arts: they are small, open infrequently, and show new blood. Taken in conjunction with a visit to the Bibliothèque Nationale or to the Parc de Bercy (p. 100; two Métro stops away) or even on its own it is a worthwhile pilgrimage for those looking to discover the current Parisian art scene. Exhibitions are not on a regular schedule; to find out more, check with the Louise Association ahead of time.

Rue du Bac
Chaillot
Champs-Élysées

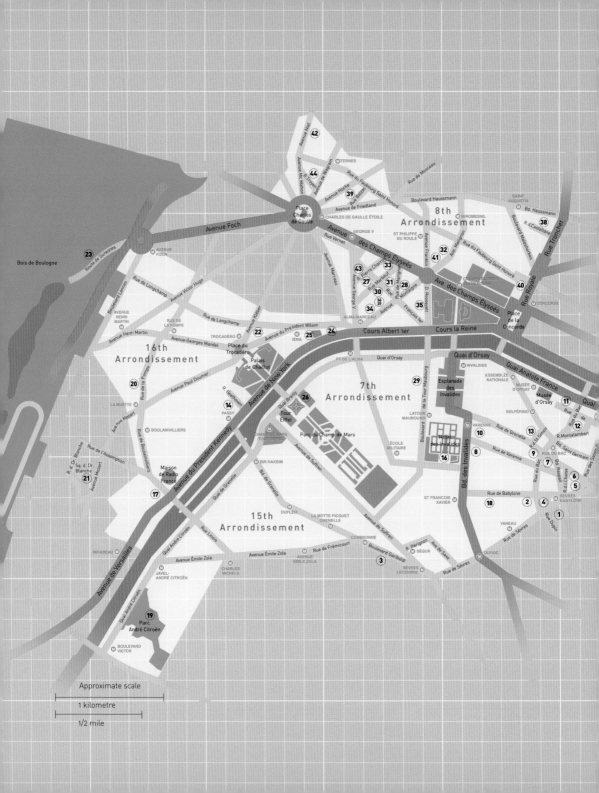

While the Right Bank can lay claim to a historic, royal air and some of the most classic and costly spots in Paris, the 7th Arrondissement has its own aristocratic attitude and luxe living, shopping and dining. An area of fine townhouses with even finer courtyard gardens, including a number of diplomatic residences, the Prime Minister's residence in the Hôtel Matignon (57 rue de Varenne), as well as government ministries, its main tourist spots are around the awe-inspiring Musée d'Orsay, Les Invalides and of course the Eiffel Tower. But the measure of the local population can be taken in the high-end design and fashion shops that cluster around the rue du Bac, leading off from the inimitable bourgeois emporium, the Bon Marché, Paris's first department store. You'll also find top-class independent French boutiques selling everything from haute eyewear to signature perfume to furnishings in retail spaces that comprise a who's who of French interior and architectural design: Philippe Starck, Christian Liaigre, Andrée Putman, Olivier de Lempeurer, Christian Biecher. While most of the grand old houses are private, one way to get an idea of what's behind the high walls is to visit the restored house-museums like the Hôtel Biron (1730), now the Musée Rodin (p. 33), and the Hôtel Bouchardon, now the Musée Maillol. There is also a highly visible antiques route that now numbers over 100 shops in the neighbourhood.

With the Eiffel Tower beckoning towards the Seine and the congestion of streets dispersing towards the southwest, a journey to the Parc André Citroën brings visitors from the small-scale perfection of the 7th to an open landscape that holds its own collection of wonders in an array of enchanting gardens: grand and airy, sculptural and poetic. If the weather is good, the detour is worth making, not least because it brings you near the gardens of another era, the Bois de Boulogne, a work of romantic 19th-century landscaping but also home to one of Paris's finest restaurants. The gastronomic tour continues, with culinary stars in the well-heeled southern 16th and around the Palais de Chaillot, where, close by, the city's largest contemporary art venue has recently been enshrined in the Palais de Tokyo, in edgy contrast to its grand surroundings.

If you're feeling deprived of chic shopping here you need only cross over on to the field of dreams that is the Champs-Élysées. Though it is constantly condemned for its unabashed overcommercialized character it still draws people in droves. Get off the boulevard itself, and you'll discover interesting cafés, knockout bars and exquisite restaurants.

1   L'Epi Dupin

11, rue Dupin

Chef François Pasteau owns one of the city's typically 'bistronomic' venues, that is, a place where one can find refined cuisine in a laid-back atmosphere. Hence the huge success of this pocket-sized restaurant near the Bon Marché: don't even think about coming without having booked your table at least a week before (especially if you want one of the tiny terrace tables in summer). His culinary signature is a mix of French and international influences (he's worked in the USA). Creative and pleasing, although the bustle isn't necessarily for everyone.

RISING STAR

2   Bamboche

15, rue de Babylone

You have probably never heard the chef's name, which is a pity, especially for him. Food writers in Paris often wonder why the Michelin guide has still not rewarded the cheerful Claude Colliot with even one tiny star. Luckily, you can take advantage of this ludicrous situation to book a table and discover a highly creative cuisine, light, clever, spicy and bold. What will you eat? One never knows, with a chef like that. But if it's the season, you mustn't miss one of his classics, the oyster ice cream in a lemon verbena sauce. This might not sound appealing but it's delicious. And the wine list is full of gems.

SIMPLE PLEASURES

3   Les Coteaux

153

PARIS'S OLDEST DEPARTMENT STORE

4   Au Bon Marché

166

DESIGNER EYES

5   Alain Mikli

74, rue des Saints-Pères

Trained as an optician, Alain Mikli started making his own frames at the age of 23. By 1983, he could count Elton John as a fan and he was soon designing frames for top fashion houses and later developed camera technology within the frames for fans like Bono and Wim Wenders. Here amid the grand fashion names of Paris, Alain Mikli has opened a boutique designed by Philippe Starck (see also p. 36), who also created some signature frames for Mikli's collection. The shop's wengé-wood boxed display cases act as a calm foil for some of the more outlandish designs, for example Issey Miyake's (see A-poc, p. 174) foldable Dragonfly frames in clear, bright red, orange or purple and Starck's pieces in his signature stand-out hues. The boutique also carries the whole Mikli collection. This shop is also the sole source for Mikli's clothing, which is on show upstairs. Mikli's clothes are funky futuristic, all reversible, and all made in Paris's 13th arrondissement. Likewise his range of special handbags, which look like heavy wood jewel-cases but are actually made of the same lightweight material, cellulose acetate, as the spec frames, with satiny or silvery cloth in the centre.

A WORLD-CLASS NOSE

6   Editions Parfums Frédéric Malle

165

COOL, CALM AND CREAMY

7   Christian Liaigre

42, rue du Bac

Known as the purveyor of 'the new French classic style', Christian Liaigre has touched some of the finer interiors known to the design world. The Hôtel Montalembert and the Mercer Hotel in New York are just two of his supremely elegant concoctions. Think chocolate-coloured wood and crisp cream upholstery, clean lines and a precious few colours for ornament and you have the essence of Liaigre's shop on the rue du Bac. Subtle, yes, but also a feast for the senses in the polish of the wood and the gentle, seductive curve of a chair. Liaigre has not only made a name for himself, he's made his own name synonymous with smooth elegance.

MUSEUM FOR AN ENIGMA

8   Le Musée Rodin

77, rue de Varenne

The Hôtel Biron was known as a fine house and garden even before Rodin took up residence, in the wake of artists like Henri Matisse and Jean Cocteau, in 1908 at the age of 68. A masterpiece of rocaille architecture completed in 1730, the house later fell on hard times but the museum has brought back much of the original décor, including, recently, some fine painted overdoors by François Lemoyne. Inside are numerous busts, drawings and paintings by Rodin and others, while in the restored gardens are such masterworks as *The Thinker*, *Ugolino*, *The Gates of Hell* and *The Burghers of Calais*.

ARTISTIC LABOUR OF LOVE

9 Fondation Dina Vierny-Musée Maillol
61, rue de Grenelle

Aristide Maillol (1861–1944) met Dina Vierny when she was 15. He was late in his career but he had been told she resembled his sculpture. She became his model and close friend until his death 10 years later. Vierny, who had also posed for Matisse and Bonnard, planned for 30 years to create a museum dedicated to an artist whose talent was not fully recognized during his lifetime. Opened in 1995, the museum contains the whole of Maillol's oeuvre, from drawings, engravings and paintings to his distinctive voluptuous sculptures, as well as pieces by contemporary artists such as Rodin, Gauguin, Picasso, Degas and Cézanne. The museum also hosts temporary exhibitions.

VEGETABLE ARTS

10 L'Arpège

144

REDEFINING ECLECTICISM

11 Epoca
60, rue de Verneuil

'My periods: from 2nd century BC (for certain archaeological pieces) to tomorrow', says Mony Linz-Einstein. Her 'strange' choices of objects, she admits, 'always provoke curiosity'. Visitors to her gallery reap the benefits of her wide-ranging taste. There are items as traditional as a set of green leather Chesterfield chairs or a blue-washed Gustavan closed bed, but then there are the old carved Indian columns, the cork champagne cabinet from Reims, the antler chandeliers, the 19th-century window surrounds and the larger-than-life carved wood statue of Hanuman, the mythical Hindu monkey ruler. It's an eccentric jumble all rather casually displayed in a large warehouse of a space, and browsing, though not touching, is encouraged.

COOLEST CASHMERE

12 Lucien Pellat-Finet

175

REGENCY REDUX

13 Hôtel Duc de Saint-Simon

130

SMALL BUT PERFECTLY FORMED

14 L'Astrance

139

ANTIQUES OF THE LEFT BANK

15 Carré Rive Gauche

In an almost perfect square bordered by the Quai Voltaire, the rue des Saints-Pères, the rue de l'Université and the rue du Bac is a collection of streets in which antiques dealers banded together in the 1970s to promote their trade and to cooperate in group exhibitions or 'open days', which now take place mainly in May. Today there are more than 100 dealers clustered into the two-square-block area, and with the cooperation of organizations abroad, the events make for a lively influx of collectors from abroad. The organization remains active all year, however, and any shop sporting a Carré Rive Gauche emblem signals its participation and experience in the serious business of collecting.

GILDED SPLENDOUR

16 Eglise-du-Dôme
Hôtel des Invalides

Soaring over the formal gardens of Les Invalides and distinguished by its elongated cupola is one of Paris's greatest Baroque architectural wonders, designed by Jules Hardouin-Mansart in 1679 and completed in 1706. If the golden presence of the dome (regilded with 12 kilos [26.5 pounds] of gold for the bicentennial of the French Revolution in 1989) doesn't lure you inside, then surely the prospect of seeing Napoleon's tomb will, despite the otherwise uncharismatic interior.

ART HOUSE

17 Hotel Square

118

ORIENTALISM PAR EXCELLENCE

18 La Pagode
57 bis, rue de Babylone

An architectural curiosity built in 1896 by the wife of the entrepreneur behind Au Bon Marché (see p. 166), the Pagode began life as a Japanese-style *petite folie* before becoming a rather exotic movie theatre in 1931. Cocteau premiered *Le Testament d'Orphée* here in 1959, and the venue was saved from demolition by director Louis Malle in the 1970s. Substantially renovated recently, today the venue features mainly alternative international films.

19 Parc André Citroën

Between quai André-Citroën, rue Leblanc,
rue de la Montagne-de-la-Fage

One feels a little like a modern-day Alice in Wonderland
here, especially when entering from the north end at rue
Cauchy and encountering the allée formed by stepped
concrete cubes wrapped in box hedges leading to a tunnel
of trees and beyond to other wonders both formal and
wild. In the land where the formal garden was invented,
it's no surprise that the 20th-century version is something
to behold. Three-storey greenhouse towers on one side of
a path are countered by small, shaded pergolas. A *jardin
en mouvement* contains bamboo and other plants that
rustle in a breeze, while other areas are planted by colour
or form, all divided by geometric low stone walls and
walks. A ramped waterfall flows into a canal that separates
the vast green playing field from the rest of the park and
is crossed by a series of small wooden bridges. The
culmination of the water, greenhouse and sculptural
stonework is the pavement fountains that dance in front
of the two great glassed conservatories. Landscape artists
Gilles Clément and Alain Provost, along with architects,
completed work in 1992 on former Citroën factory land.
Until the Bercy park (see. p. 100) was completed, it was the
largest Parisian park project of the 20th century.

(see. p. 100)

DESIGN-GASTRONOMIC COLLABORATION

20 Bon

25, rue de la Pompe

When international superstar designer Philippe Starck
and hip restaurateur Laurent Taïeb (see also p. 84) opened
this huge eatery, numerous food writers (for once
unanimous) had a great laugh, for Bon (an acronym for
'biological, organic, natural') did not appear to be *bon*
(good) at all. But things have clearly changed since
Bordeaux chef Jean-Marie Amat recently took over the
kitchen. You can now have more than decent, if rather
expensive meals (try the tuna with a coffee-peanut gravy)
in what remains one of Paris's most exuberant and brilliant
nouveau-Baroque décors, with a cosy boudoir, Zen garden,
a giant table topped with candelabras, a rhinoceros's head
on top of a chimney – and much, much more.

(see also p. 84)

21 Fondation Le Corbusier
8–10, square du Docteur-Blanche

If you claim to have any interest in the birth of modern design then a visit to this collection is a must, as it houses the complete notes on the life and work of one of the most influential architects of the 20th century. The Villa La Roche and Villa Jeanneret, both designed by the visionary architect, are home to Le Corbusier's drawings, plans and artworks, which he bequeathed, on his death in 1965, with the aim of keeping them together as a comprehensive body of work. The Fondation has done just that, making it available to the public in its entirety as well as holding periodic exhibitions. Furniture he designed alone and in collaboration with Pierre Jeanneret and Charlotte Perriand is also on display. The houses themselves, built in 1923, are prime examples of his early buildings.

FABULOUS FUSIONS
22 Passiflore
33, rue de Longchamp

Chef Roland Durand often describes himself as a peasant traveller. He does not want to choose between flavours from here or there, between French or Thai fragrances, spices from India or cheese from the Auvergne, where he was born. Hence his intriguing cuisine manages excitingly to combine what he learnt in France with what he discovered abroad, especially in Asia, mixing modern with traditional, classic with exotic. Soups and mushrooms are his passions and never absent from the menu. The wine list is as singular as the dishes and the décor is both cosy and exotic.

SYLVAN SPLENDOUR
23 Le Pré Catalan
141

TWO-STAR APPLE
24 6 New York
6, avenue de New-York

The first good reason to come here is that the place is simply beautiful, contemporarily designed, with crockery by Dior and warm, golden-beige panelling. Though fewer tables would afford more privacy, this brand-new venue run by Jean-Pierre Vigato (a two-star chef from Apicius)

is starting to be regarded as a clever, modern restaurant offering light and delicate 'pizzaletas' with langoustines and spinach, as well as a 100% rustic-chic pork plate and an unmissable tiramisù. It's quite expensive but most clients seem to come conveniently armed with AmEx Business Platinum cards.

MODERN ART UPDATE
25 Palais de Tokyo
13, avenue du Président-Wilson

The Musée d'Art Moderne already occupied one wing of the large, neo-classical Palais de Tokyo, built in 1937, but the need for 'flexible space in which to present international art', according to Palais directors Jérôme Sans and Nicolas Bourriaud, was the driving force behind the new interior designed by competition-winners Anne Lacaton and Jean-Philippe Vassal. And versatile is certainly one word for it, and dynamic industrial are two more. The new work is invisible from the outside, apart from the giant, semi-transparent portraits hung in each of the window openings, but inside the architects have created something akin to an open-plan artist's loft space by ripping out beams, floors and other obstructions to create a hangar-like backdrop for all size and manner of exhibitions, which are open from noon until midnight. The bookshop is enclosed by a chain-link fence, keeping up the temporary-construction theme. Downstairs the tabula rasa has been livened up in the colourful café area that spills out on to the terrace, where the hillside site becomes apparent and a view over the Seine is art of a different nature.

NEW HEIGHTS OF CUISINE
26 Jules Verne
137

HALL OF FAME
27 Pershing Hall
124

GLOBAL FUSION COMES TO PARIS
28 Spoon, Food & Wine
138

TASTE TEASERS
29 Petrossian
143

30 La Masion de l'Aubrac

37, rue Marbeuf

31 Courrèges

40, rue François-ler

Beef at three in the morning? Why should that sound eccentric? Especially if the meat comes straight from the Aubrac region, where the owner's family breeds this exquisite cattle. Many Parisian chefs know it and gather here after closing their own restaurants. Night owls, taxi drivers, lost tourists and beef worshippers know it too: thus, the place is frequently overcrowded and the welcome may be less than wholehearted. If that should happen, here's how to recover: call one of the two young sommeliers, check the amazing wine list (900 references) and let them help you find an absorbingly interesting bottle from Languedoc-Roussillon or the Rhône valley. Then just sit back, relax and watch the sun rise.

First opened in 1965, Courrèges boutique of the 21st century has the space-age pure white and lucite décor that has both a futuristic and slightly retro feel, especially in the context of the go-go miniskirts, squared, above-the-knee shift dresses in window-pane checks, zippered white boots and bags, all looking slightly familiar but also very chic. Courrèges seems to have been suspended perfectly in time, except for the updated young shop assistants. Its pure aesthetic has the effect of making shoppers look like less-perfect intrusions. The Café Blanc next door is as shiny white and just as haughty.

LIAIGRE MEETS VONG

32 Market

15, avenue Matignon

CARS AND COCKTAILS

33 Atelier Renault

53, avenue des Champs-Élysées

With all the restaurants he has launched in the past ten years, from New York to Las Vegas, Hong Kong to Chicago, one might have thought Jean-Georges Vongerichten (born and raised in Alsace) would never come back to his homeland. He finally did, with the help of Christie's chairman François Pinault and film director Luc Besson. Designer Christian Liaigre (see p. 33) has turned Market into a refined, Asian-inspired place, whose interior in beige tints and wood matches the Thai-French fare rather well. Although meals are perhaps more relaxed that those who have tried Jean-Georges's cuisine elsewhere, an excellent wine list and service and chic clientele make it all worthwhile.

The grand processional boulevard is now known more for its expensive boutiques and outdoor café seating than for parades of state. Among the former, the Renault showroom and café-bar, one of Paris's newest cultural destinations, has to be one of the most innovative and fun. Shiny new models poised on the ground floor and tilted up on the wall are accompanied by loops of racing video. A small café area is set apart from the cars downstairs while a bar upstairs covered in chic metal mesh signals the racy, fashionable side of car culture. A lounge area has cool, funnel-shaped, grey leather chairs and there are tables laid out along a mezzanine catwalk spanning the entrance area and another a half level higher across the front window is possibly one of the most desirable *indoor* seats in the neighbourhood.

THE VIEW FROM ON HIGH
34 La Maison Blanche
15, avenue Montaigne

Among the trendiest restaurants of the moment is the famous Maison Blanche, situated on the roof of one of the smartest theatres in town, the Théâtre des Champs-Élysées. The buzz got a boost when Jacques and Laurent Pourcel, the three-star twins from Montpellier, decided to take control of the place, redecorating it with works by one of Starck's disciples and bringing to Paris their reinvented southern cuisine (often funky and tasty, most of the time atrociously expensive). Try to get a table near the huge *baie vitrée* (you will gasp when you see the amazing view over the city) or in one of the cosy, intimate and colourful boxes.

RENEWED CLASSIC
35 Lasserre
147

GRAND PERFECTION
36 Alain Ducasse at the Plaza-Athénée
145

MODELS ON ICE
37 Bar at the Plaza-Athénée
155

IN THE NAMES
38 Au Coin de la Rue
10, rue de Castellane

Perhaps for a start a few names – Jean Nouvel, Ron Arad, Yamakado, Hugues Chevalier. This is a place that is much more original and modern than the name suggests ('au coin de la rue' meaning 'on the corner of the street'). It has quickly become one of the city's most modern and creative eateries, each designer or architect having brought his individual touch to the structure, the lighting, the garden, the furniture. Moreover, since one of the partners is the famous auctioneer Jacques Tajan, you may make bids while you casually snack on a tuna carpacccio with mango.

SURPRISING DELIGHTS
39 Pierre Gagnaire
142

BRIGHT LIGHTS IN THE CITY
40 La Cantine du Faubourg
157

HIP EXOTICA
41 Nirvana
158

WINE BAR TRÈS CHIC
42 Les Caves Pétrissans
30 bis, avenue Niel

There are some wine bars where you bump into more Hermès ties than Nikes: Les Caves Pétrissans, with its chic atmosphere and clientele, is one of them. But you'll never feel uncomfortable, since conviviality is this bistro's buzzword and people of all kinds rub shoulders around the bar. The décor (worth a visit in itself) is as ageless as the food – perfect bistro and home-cooking fare with set pieces of steak tartare (superb), calf's head with shallot sauce, kidneys, to name a few. And since the place doubles as a vintner's, have a look at the remarkable wine list and then you can go next door and buy a bottle of your own.

BAD BOY IN THE NEIGHBOURHOOD
43 Jean Paul Gaultier
44, avenue George V

There was a time when the Breton-shirt-wearing designer was considered something of a shock-monger. But today Gaultier is almost as fashion establishment as Dior. Thankfully, this doesn't mean that the former *enfant terrible* is resting on his laurels. In October of 2002, the ever-active Gaultier upped sticks from a fantastically designed (and not very old) shop space in the edgy Bastille neighbourhood and settled in, to some amount of high-class fanfare, on one of the princely avenues of the 8th arrondissement. Fetish-clad mannequins bestride something like lampposts and mirror-framed video loops of catwalk footage and some fantasy-inspired lighting are all visible through the clear glass frontage (the previous shop windows were teasingly obscured) but that's only the front room. Enter at your own risk.

SIMPLY LUXURIOUS
44 Guy Savoy
134

Right Bank
Palais-Royal
Montorgueil

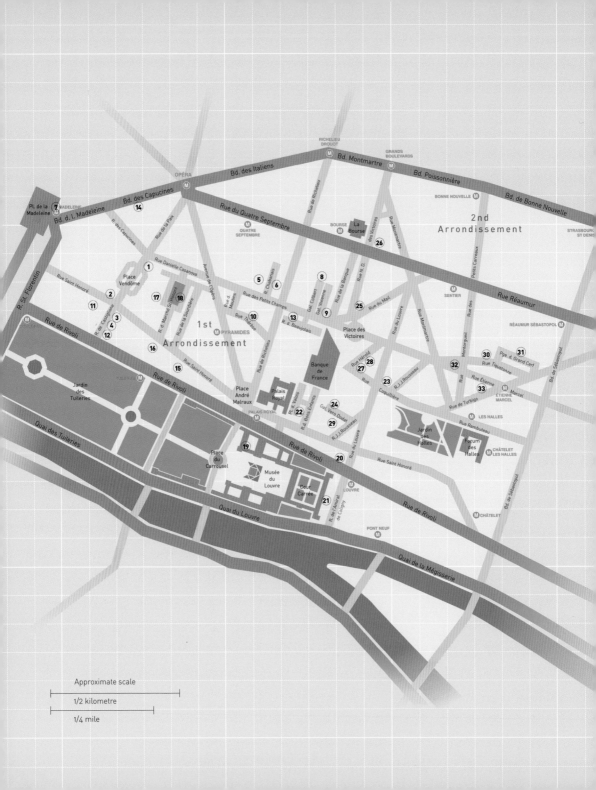

The spiral of arrondissements, as conceived in the 19th century by urban planner extraordinary Baron Haussmann, begins here, in the quarter dominated by the grand architectural spectacle of the Louvre, the Louvre itself and the Tuileries taking up most of the riverfront. This is still the heart of visitors' Paris, not as it was in the days when the Louvre was still a palace and Les Halles was a thriving marketplace, but a historic beating heart to which people are drawn for a glimpse of the Belle Époque and the ancien régime. When not held in thrall in the Louvre or the Museum of Decorative Arts, people come here for star-quality shopping, eating and drinking. Some old and traditional, and some new and equally grand spots off the Place Vendôme whisper to your pocketbook, as do the restaurants and bars, the oldest of which, Le Grand Véfour (1760, p. 136), will take your breath away with its décor. Modern-day masters of grandeur, the Costes brothers, Gilbert and Jean-Louis, who ratcheted up the design of Parisian restaurant-bars with their first, Café Costes (in collaboration with Philippe Starck) in 1984, have created the stylish Café Marly (p. 151) overlooking I.M. Pei's glass pyramids at the Louvre and have pulled out all the Empire stops along with the flamboyant design of Jacques Garcia at the Hôtel Costes (p. 159).

A less modern extravagance is to be had in the *galeries*. These beautifully designed 19th-century covered passages were created to promote the fashionable Belle Époque activity of shopping. It was a time when Napoleon III's empress Eugénie led the nation, or at least the nouveau riches, in a taste for conspicuous consumption, which at the end of the 20th century has culminated in the birth of the 'concept store', where art, design and fashion meet to form a holistic experience. Today shops like Colette (p. 50) and Castelbajac (p. 51), as well as design-conscious Comme des Garçons (p. 51) and Mandarina Duck (p. 50), have made the experience of being inside the shop as important as the articles to be purchased.

The attempts to revive the fortunes of Les Halles, the centuries-old market, later enclosed by Napoleon III and replaced in the 1970s with a universally unloved complex, have not achieved continued success. Though the surrounding area is probably no less savoury than it has been for centuries, somehow the modern intrusion makes it that much more avoidable. But one only has to go a little farther north to the small pedestrianized streets of Montorgueil, around rue Tiquetonne and Étienne-Marcel, to find cool and funky in a slightly more salubrious setting.

1 Charvet

28, place Vendôme

'Trendy' is not a word you associate with this, one of Paris's last surviving traditional shirtmakers, but if you are looking for something with that quintessential Paris gentlemanly air then this venerable old institution is a worthwhile stop. Made-to-measure shirts (still sewn one at a time in their workshop) as well as ties and handkerchiefs in dozens of fabrics and patterns, a selection of classic pyjamas and toiletries are all on display in the reassuringly old-fashioned premises. The inventor of removable collars and cuffs, Charles Charvet opened up in 1838 and was soon shirtmaker to royalty and nouveau riche alike.

HOMAGE TO THE SUN KING

2 Hôtel de Vendôme

116

BIJOUX PERFUME

3 JAR

165

SEXY STILETTOS

4 Rodolphe Ménudier

171

EXOTIC NATURAL FIBRES

5 CMO

5, rue Chabanais

Lampshades, rugs and accessories made from woven pineapple fibres, nettles and water hyacinths are just some of the unusual delights that Corinne Muller and Marianne Oudin stock in their popular and highly eco-friendly shop. A whole range of different plant fibres are used by the designers to create unusual textiles, which they then dye themselves to achieve objects and fabrics of startling and startlingly natural beauty. You can also order their fabrics in lengths, as with regular woven materials, for your own upholstery, shades or wall coverings. They've become a favourite of modern designers looking for a distinctive natural texture and vivid hues.

WINE AND SCOTS

6 Juvenile's

47, rue de Richelieu

You might not want to come to Paris to meet English-speaking tourists. But what you might want to find is a wily wine bar, even if it's run by a Scot called Tim Johnston. Therefore, seize the occasion to ask the owner (in English, obviously) what's worth looking at from the French vineyards. He might have you start with a glass of Purple Four (a Rhône valley vintage specially blended for him), then take you to the Barossa valley (the international wine list is clever, though a bit expensive). Meanwhile, you'll be pecking at some nice tapas (hot chorizo included) or cheese plates. Wine can also be purchased to take home.

ART AND CUISINE NOUVEAU

7 Lucas-Carton

140

POSH PROMENADE

8 Galerie Vivienne

4, rue des Petits-Champs, rue Vivienne
• Jean Paul Gaultier, no. 6
• A Priori Thé, nos 35–37
• Christain Astuguevieille, no. 42

Parisian covered passages are a delight to discover, particularly on a rainy day. But the 19th-century Galerie Vivienne, being in the posh 2nd arrondissement, offers a lavish sort of shopping and shelter. The grand arcade is home to Jean Paul Gaultier's masterpiece of a retail space, some fine stalls of books and prints and the lovely A Priori Thé for afternoon refreshment. Artist, furniture designer and fragrance adviser to Comme des Garçons, Christian Astuguevieille has an outlet here for his signature creations – chairs and chests of drawers in painted hemp cord and unbarked chestnut, as well as his sculpture and pen-and-ink drawings.

CLASSIC WINE SHOP

9 Legrand Filles et Fils

152

BOXING CLEVER

10 Claude Jeantet

10, rue Thérèse

Though most of her creations were never boxes, architect Claude Jeantet's cardboard curiosities have that appeal of humble materials being put to somewhat loftier use. Delightful dogs, cats and rabbits appear alongside useful household items like picture frames and copies of the artist's book on how to do it yourself with cardboard. She also uses other base materials, like sponge. All in this enchanting little box of a shop.

In the arena of haute jewelry that is the Vendôme, Ida Faerber's tiny antique jewelry shop is a gem, lined with luxurious light-burgundy velvet. Faerber sources and sells jewelry mainly from the 19th-century and Art Déco periods. Like many premiere jewellers, Ida Faerber doesn't advertise – though she does welcome visitors through the door.

The Italian company's flagship Paris store is a visual delight. The space is animated by a series of displays – swirling, bending structures all brightly coloured, lit and textured – that orbit around the 'rotating spiral stair'. With a reputable line of leather goods and clothing, Mandarina Duck has achieved with its sleek-designed, lightweight nylon travel bags a near cult following. Add to that the array of unique hues that can be matched in sets or mixed up like a Mondrian and you see why the Italians never give in to the idea that practical has to be prosaic.

The woman who created this early 'concept store', mixing design, art fashion and books on the subjects in a high-design backdrop, did it fashionably on a first-name basis. Now when such holistic blends have become much more commonplace, Colette still holds the reins with this original and still top-notch fashion emporium. The three floors of minimally designed premises feature an international

collection of clothing and accessories, art objects, electronic gadgetry and cosmetics from the pantheon of designers. Downstairs everything from designer furniture to toiletries is on offer, as well as a restaurant and the refreshment of the famed 'water bar', where you can sample from around 80 brands from all over the globe. Despite its high profile, this is a shop where browsing is part of the experience, with a photo gallery and bookshop on the mezzanine level, as well as space for temporary exhibitions.

SIMPLE SCENTS

17 Comme des Garçons Parfums

164

DESIGNERLY SQUARE

18 Place du Marché-Saint-Honoré
- Philippe Modal, no. 33
- Castelbajac, no. 31

The 1st arrondissement has an abundance of opulent retail spaces but this small *place*, dominated by the looming glass office building at its centre, boasts several creative gems. Extravagant milliner turned home furnishings designer Philippe Modal has one of his larger premises at 33. Nearly opposite is a Castelbajac 'concept store' where clothes and art meet.

MUSEUM OPULENCE

19 Le Café Marly

151

CAPITAL ANTIQUES

20 Louvre des Antiquaires
2, place du Palais-Royal

If you're looking for traditional period antiques from Louis XV to 19th-century Russian to Sèvres porcelain, what better neighbourhood to peruse than that of the Louvre. Originally founded in 1855 by Messrs Chauchard and Hériot as the Grands Magasins du Louvre, it was the first shop of its kind in Paris. Today 250 dealers are arranged on three levels in this mall-like structure across the rue de Rivoli from the Louvre. Because dealers sign a document that obliges them to respect certain rules regarding the age and quality of their objects, they are subject to random and unannounced quality-control checks by experts, thus ensuring that the quality is high and the dealers are reputable. It might not fit everyone's pocketbook, but you can always bargain, especially if you're paying in cash and your French is good enough for haggling.

21 Le Fumoir

6, rue de l'Amiral-de-Coligny

22 Patrick Fourtin

9, rue des Bons-Enfants

The family behind the China Club's colonial chic (p. 158) created Le Fumoir in a similar style, complete with slow-turning ceiling fans. It's a café, bar and restaurant that combines the look and feel of a gentleman's club library with a smooth, 1930s-inspired décor. The location is hard to beat, opposite the Cour Carrée du Louvre but off the main drag of the rue de Rivoli, with a few tables outside and some just inside the door, where people lounge and read the newspaper or the Fumoir's own literary review. The bar is a great old-fashioned wood-and-mirror affair, a sign of a serious drinks list. Farther inside it becomes more like a restaurant, with ordered tables and a fusion-style menu. The library is where everyone wants to be, but any seat you manage to get – and this could prove difficult – won't disappoint.

Selling mostly furniture and objects from the 1930s, 1940s and 1950s, Patrick Fourtin has made a name for himself as a purveyor of modern French design. Some of his favoured creators include André Arbus, Gilbert Poillerat, Jacques Adnet and Rollin. 'Occasionally we will have something from the 19th century,' says co-gallerist Roberto Ardone, 'perhaps a great Italian mirror, to show that you can have a space that is not fixed in a particular period.' As proof of this they also try to arrange the gallery 'as if it were a private house', with a mixture of styles and periods. The shop also occasionally hosts exhibitions. As the French 1940s hot up for collectors, Patrick Fourtin is all aglow.

23 La Cloche des Halles
28, rue Coquillière

It's best to avoid this wonderful place at lunchtime, when white-collar and other workers pour in to occupy the tiny tables. For this funny little bistro is one of the best cheap bites of the neighbourhood and a classic wine bar of Les Halles since many a year (the owner, Serge Lesage, still bottles his fine Beaujolais himself). Farm cheeses are perfect (don't miss the Cantal), as well as all the pork classics (white ham and country ham, jambon persillé with its parsleyed aspic and many varieties of sausages). Like going back to the 1950s.

24 Galerie du Passage
20–22, passage Véro-Dodat

This lovely covered passage dates from 1826 and retains its original mahogany panelling, decorative columns and friezes and diamond-patterned tile floor. Like many Parisian *galeries*, it was something of a precursor to a modern mall but obviously much more picturesque. The Galerie du Passage, run by Pierre Passbon, is a highlight among the antiques and vintage shops here. Specializing in French furnishings of the the 20th century, he counts Alexandre Noll, Jean-Michel Franck and Christian Bérard among his well-chosen collection.

A LITTLE ROMANCE
27 Sandrine Philippe

6, rue Hérold

In an area where flashy designs and even flashier retail spaces practically leap out at you it is refreshing to find such understated glamour. 'I make clothes with a story, a history,' says the softspoken young designer who worked for the house of Courrèges before starting her own label in 1997. She aims for designs that are old-fashioned, which for Philippe means 'poetic and feminine'. Using the cottons, silks and wools that she then customizes with 'dyeing, burning, painting and artisanal applications', she makes clothes that are uniquely soft, romantic and sophisticated. The shop reflects a marriage of romance and cool aesthetic, its concrete floor set off with recessed flowers and violet walls hung with delicate jewelry. Her approach is the opposite of shock value: 'I want customers to feel something with these garments,' Philippe explains, 'like they have always known them'.

SHOE FETISH
29 Christian Louboutin

175

FASHION BY WEIGHT
30 Killiwatch

64, rue Tiquetonne

Encapsulating the trend-setting vibe that the streets around Etienne-Marcel have established in recent years is rue Tiquetonne, a narrow street filled with boutiques, little restaurants and workshops, all cheek by jowl. One of the first catalysts of the area is Killiwatch, which presents the designer and second-hand street fashions. Begun 15 years ago as a second-hand and 'remade' second-hand shop, Killiwatch boasts over a dozen shops in Japan and several outside of Paris, dubbed 'Kilo-shops' where second-hand clothes are sold by the kilo. This outlet has been around for nearly seven years and its popularity only seems to increase, even though they no longer sell their own brand. Jeans, tops and sport shoes from an international roster of street-fashion designers from Diesel and Pépé to Swedish line Redwood, 60 in all to choose from, while you struggle to make yourself look as cool as the staff.

THE GRAND OLD DAYS
31 Passage du Grand Cerf
- La Corbeille, no. 5 (2nd floor)
- PM & Co, no. 5
- As'Art, no. 3
- Marie-Lise Goëlo, no. 10
- Jean-Louis Pinabel, no. 4

The pretty wrought-ironwork of this unusually tall, light-filled passage, built around 1835, is only part of its charm. Running between rue St-Denis and rue Dussoubs and parallel to the small, design-filled rue Tiquetonne, the Passage du Grand Cerf provides a Belle Époque setting for modern design flair and funky fashion accessories. La Corbeille is a haven for fine finds from the 1950s to the present. Pierre Paulin, Charles and Ray Eames, Eero Saarinen and Olivier Mourgue stand proud as the classics that they are among a host of objects and lighting that are slightly more whimsical but never tacky. For another time and another era, have a look in at the new Asian-inspired designs at PM & Co. As'Art presents ethnic and African pieces made by contemporary designers. Marie-Lise Goëlo is a jeweller who specializes in costume pieces, while Jean-Louis Pinabel makes lively hats whose feathered touches hark back to the 1930s and 1950s.

COSTES CONTINUUM
32 Étienne-Marcel
34, rue Étienne-Marcel

Where Café Marly was the success of the 1990s, the success of the Y2Ks is likely to be this café with no name on its façade, the latest opening from the Costes brothers. The décor, all vivid primary colours, set off by white, with a floor covering made of artistic scribble, is the result of a collaboration between artist Pierre Huyghe and *Vogue* art directors and graphic designers Mathias Augustyniak and Michael Amzalag, otherwise known as M/M. The atmosphere has a certain aesthetic inclination towards the 1970s, something between *A Clockwork Orange* and *2001, A Space Odyssey*, with lots of plastic fantastic. Being a Costes collaboration, this is a place to see and be seen, at least while the novelty shines bright.

FANCIFUL FINISHING TOUCHES
33 Declercq Passementiers
15, rue Étienne-Marcel

Once you have splashed out for some fantastic fabrics at Dominique Kieffer (p. 173) you can head around the corner to this temple to tassels and trims. If the French have the patent on dramatic period interior, then this is where you find the blueprints, or at least some of the key ingredients for embellishing a hem, gathering a swag or tying off a grand drapery in true Parisian style.

Grands Boulevards
Pigalle
Montmartre

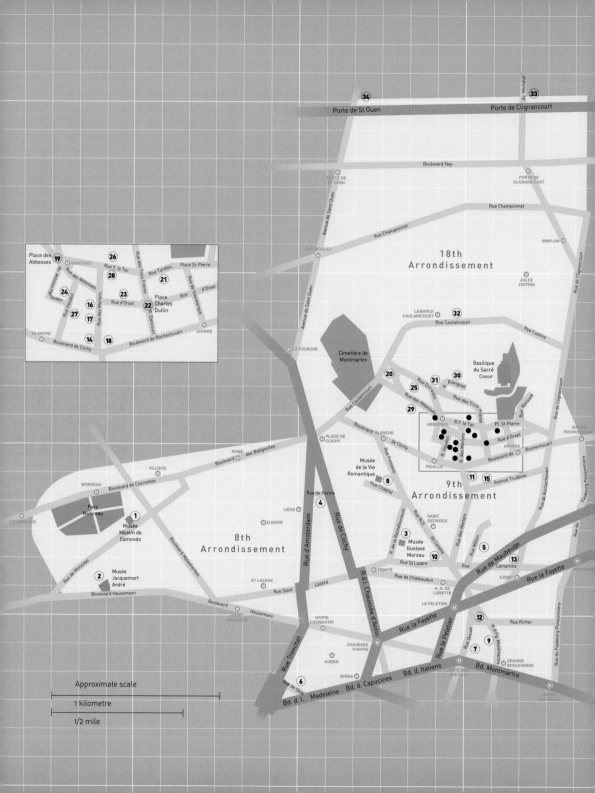

The great thoroughfares were first laid out as tree-lined avenues by Louis XIV and widened to Empire proportions by Napoleon's urban modernizer Baron Haussmann in the 19th century. Despite periods of neglect those grand boulevards, lined as they are by great houses, maintain the poise of an area that was in the late 19th century the height of fashion. Around the same time, when the boulevards were patrolled by carriage or on foot by those with an urge to see and be seen, the 9th arrondissement was dubbed the 'Nouvelle-Athènes', taking its name from its neo-classical buildings but also from the group of artists and writers who converged in literary and artistic salons here. The Musée de la Vie Romantique (p. 65) provides an atmospheric snapshot of the creative period peopled by such characters as Eugène Delacroix, Frédéric Chopin and George Sand, as does another artistic house-museum, the Musée Gustave Moreau (p. 62). Though many streets are now unremarkable, the grandeur epitomized by the boulevards and the extravagant Second Empire Opéra Garnier still exists in pockets around the 9th, as does a certain subtle artistic flavour. Pigalle, another formerly artistic neighbourhood, eases into the renowned conglomeration of art and licence that is Montmartre by way of the rue des Martyrs, known today more for its mix of new and bohemian fashions than for its sacrificial history.

La Butte, as it is known to Parisians, meaning the 'hill' or 'mound', refers to the place where St Denis was decapitated by Romans in the 3rd century. It was later called Mons Martyrum, which evolved to Montmartre. By the 18th century, as Haussmann ploughed through the heart of Paris, Montmartre remained a village idyll, with thatched cottages, windmills (*moulins*) and vineyards. Artists Renoir, Braque, Van Gogh, Dufy and, of course, Toulouse-Lautrec began filing in to the preserved rural corner. Utrillo was a native and painted some of the most evocative scenes of his home turf, but it was Toulouse-Lautrec's various tributes to the great Moulin Rouge, which opened in 1889, and its musical stars like Jane Avril that put Montmartre on the tourist map. Today, artistic creativity is once again booming in Montmartre but not in the 'artist'-filled Place du Tertre. Individual boutiques selling everything from antiques to handmade jewelry and fabrics to modern furniture and new designs, as well as the requisite art galleries, are flourishing anew in the southern section around rue des Abbesses and Place Charles-Dullin. The best bars, pubs and cafés are those that manage to preserve some of the historic and romantic associations together with a modern attitude. But if the romance of years past is in your heart, head north to the flea-market 'village' of Saint-Ouen to buy a piece of history.

1 Le Musée Nissim de Camondo

63, rue de Monceau

For a museum whose treasures came from a family who knew such tragedy, the Musée Nissim de Camondo is surprisingly exuberant, a celebration of 18th-century French decoration and craftsmanship. Jacob, Sèvres, Meissen, Huet and a host of other names linked to the golden age of French decoration fill the meticulously laid-out rooms. The banking family de Camondo were known as 'the Rothschilds of the East', coming from Constantinople to establish branches in Paris. It was Moïse de Camondo who tore down the family house on this site in 1910 and had a new building erected, inspired by the Petit Trianon at Versailles. The museum is named for his son, Nissim, who was killed in the First World War. His daughter, Béatrice, was later deported by the Nazis along with her husband and children and died at Auschwitz.

OPULENT HOUSE MUSEUM

2 Musée Jacquemart André

158, boulevard Haussmann

Their subtitle is 'the most sumptuous residence in Paris' and it's not all hyperbole, though it is rather overwhelming. Edouard André was head of a great banking family and already an art collector when he met Nélie Jacquemart, who was commissioned to paint his portrait. Together they amassed a collection of works by some of the world's best-known artists and exhibited them in their exquisitely decorated mansion built in 1875. The many rooms are kept generally as they were before Nélie died and bequeathed the collection to the state in 1913, but as the couple's tastes ran to historic opulence, so does the museum today. Many rooms are spectacular in their own right, but together they make for an astounding display of grandeur. Works by David, Boucher, Chardin and Fragonard are among the treasures in the French collection. The pair also had a great fondness for Italian and Dutch painting. Tapestries, furniture and objects in the private and grand 'informal' apartments are also displayed in stunning Louis XV and Empire settings. The spectacular tea-room, a destination in its own right, is housed in the former dining room, which is draped in red velvet and boasts a ceiling painted by Tiepolo and Brussels tapestries.

HOUSE OF ART

3 Musée Gustave Moreau

14, rue de La Rochefoucauld

Born in Paris in 1826, Gustave Moreau was a prolific painter who helped to usher in the Symbolist and Surrealist movements. He worked with great intensity while living alone in his family house, and much of his work was seen only by close friends. But Moreau intended that the house and studio should be preserved as a museum and arranged its contents so that they would 'give a small idea of the person I was and the atmosphere in which I liked to dream'. Thousands of works, from delicate sketches of animals and plants to monumental canvases depicting scenes from the Bible, myth and fantasy, are displayed in two large, light-filled studio rooms joined by a spiral iron staircase. Domestic rooms, including one devoted to his student and mistress, present an intriguing glimpse of late-19th-century French bourgeois life.

COOL COMFORTS

4 Pavillon de Paris

128

UNIQUE GALLERY

5 L'Œil du Huit

8, rue Milton

In the spirit of the Moreau Museum, this simple little gallery is the brainchild and life work of Emmanuelle Gutierres Requenne, who has a studio in the back and opened up the place in 1997 to have 'the sort of gallery I would like to show my own work in'. She performs this service now for a number of local and French artists, whose work she rotates in a series of one-person exhibitions. Requenne's taste is for new and interesting art that doesn't necessarily leap out from the white-walled industrial space, but does draw visitors in. Between visits to Detaille (p. 66) and a spot of lunch at Velly (p. 67), it makes for a nice, artistic aside.

6 Cojean

4, rue de Sèze

If you're on your knees after a shopping spree at the Conran Shop or looking for something marginally healthy to eat and drink, you will be pleasantly satisfied at Cojean, where home-made sandwiches, wraps, soups, salads, trendy milk-shakes and other such quick bites offer hearty nourishment without the long haul of a full lunch. But this isn't just fast food. With a salmon tortilla or an elegant *taboulé* accompanied by a glass of danish Vooswater (expensive but great for your body and soul, if you trust the label), you can relax while browsing and be invigorated by the latest issue of *Vogue* in a light-blue ultra-clean setting and pleasant staff (dressed in matching light-blue T-shirts).

7 Mairie du 9e

Salle Rossini, Salons Aguado
6, rue Drouot

While you're making the circuit of the antiques shops around the Drouot auction house or waiting around for the opening of the auctions at 2 pm, it's worth a small detour to stop in at the town hall, not to register, but to see the charming period rooms of the 18th-century mansion that have recently been opened as gallery space for art exhibitions, some held in conjunction with the Hôtel Drouot. As you enter the courtyard, a straight walk down the drive leads to the centre building whose circular entrance-hall ceiling has been splendidly repainted with its coloured flower decoration.

NOTES FROM THE 'NEW ATHENS'

8 Musée de la Vie Romantique

16, rue Chaptal

The museum is not about love or even love letters, it is mostly filled with objects and furniture belonging to George Sand. It was Ary Scheffer, however, court painter to Louis Philippe, who actually lived in the house and ran a salon, which was attended by the likes of Frédéric Chopin, Eugène Delacroix, Jean-Auguste Ingres and Franz Liszt, Gustave Moreau (whose own house was turned into a museum, p. 62), as well as Chopin's lover, Sand. It is the period more than the art that is celebrated here, a time when the area was known as the 'Nouvelle Athènes' because of the high concentration of artistic-philosophical minds and a certain modern spirit of enlightenment that they represented in a quarter attractive for its greenery and low-cost rentals, a seeming artistic paradise in the city. Sand's personal furnishings and memorabilia present a picture of an intellectual 19th-century household, with decorations and trinkets meant to evoke an aura of art and idealism. With Scheffer's own paintings in the reproduced period interiors and the country-style enclosed garden, it's almost possible to close your eyes and hear the music of inspiration and the emphatic conversation wafting through the rooms, truly the stuff of romance.

OLD PARISIAN STAND-BY
9   Chartier
7, rue du Faubourg-Montmartre

Where can you meet retired couples having lunch right
next to excited Japanese tourists? Where can you find
Paris's cheapest eggs mayonnaise? Chartier, of course,
and nowhere else. The menu features the last bouillon to
be found in the city, an ageless institution that'll whisk you
back a hundred years, when labourers could eat for next
to nothing in an immense Belle Époque cafeteria-like
atmosphere. Nothing much has changed since: the same
bustling waiters writing the bill on the paper tablecloth, the
same classic French fare (but definitely no great
gastronomic experience!), same prices, same noise, same
beauty. Chartier is a magnificent relic, to be treasured.

SERIOUS BEAUTY PRODUCTS
10   Detaille
10, rue St-Lazare

The cosmetics line started in 1910 with a face cream made
for women riding in the first automobiles, who had to
deal with open-air conditions and plagues of dust. Madame
Detaille, for whom the cream was made, went on to market
it from her home, along with a growing selection of new
products that are still seen by many women as beauty
essentials, like the all-natural rice powder in pure white
and other tones. In reassuringly old-fashioned wood-lined
shop premises Detaille has the air of consummate
professionalism.

VINTAGE NOSTALGIA
11   Et puis c'est tout
72, rue des Martyrs

As the rue des Martyrs marches up towards the
increasingly trendy and craft-filled lanes of Montmartre,
this small gallery of modern and retro furnishings, lighting
and objects is bound to distract you from your walk. It is
not the streamlined mid-century tables, chairs, desks and
lamps, though they are some fine pieces, that are the
most striking but the other side of creative world, the
collections of branded items like Ricard crockery, as well
as glasses, ash trays, and serving trays stamped with
vintage French product trademarks. Vincent Venen, who
runs the shop along with his wife, Michèle, buys
internationally but specializes in French designs from
the 1950s, 1960s and 1970s, setting him apart from your
average mid-century sources.

12 La Mère de Famille

35, rue du Faubourg-Montmartre

Another stop on the Drouot route, this beautiful old-fashioned shop-front shows a date of 1761 but the interior is wonderfully 19th-century, selling biscuits, chocolates and cordials in the lovely packaging that the French love to bestow on little luxuries, and sweets in gleaming little glass jars. The paintwork on La Mère de Famille is slightly more worn than you'll find in the grander shops of the Marais or St Germain des Prés but, as the name suggests, the atmosphere is also that much more comforting.

RETRO CAFÉ

13 Velly

52, rue Lamartine

Those who are interested in 1930s lighting will love this tiny red bistro, located next to one of the bo-bo (bohemian bourgeois) headquarters, the rue des Martyrs. But the lights are not the only reason you'll come here. Chef Alain Brigant is one of Paris's discreet young talents, whose maxim might be 'great cooking, decent prices'. His menus change as often as possible, so just try what comes along – the tomato millefeuille with ricotta, the beef fillet with herb emulsion, the veal in a blackcurrant sauce or the chocolate cake. You cannot fail to enjoy it. Short and interesting wine list.

WORLD MUSIC AND CHEAP DRINKS

14 Le Divan du Monde

75, rue des Martyrs

Along the ever-happening rue des Martyrs and conveniently located across the street from the art-and-music crowds' favourite café, La Fourmi (see p. 68), this club is on everybody's list for wide-ranging music in a laid-back setting, cheap drinks and great atmosphere energized by its former life as a cabaret. Featuring everything from Brazilian and Cuban and reggae to techno-pop, this likeable venue extends a warm welcome to Paris clubland. Check the website if you're in the mood for something in particular. Otherwise just go along and enjoy the live acts or watch the DJs working a mixed crowd until 5 am.

15 Gilles Oudin
Métiers d'Art et d'Industrie
20, avenue de Trudaine

Among the many antiques galleries in the 9th arrondissement Gilles Oudin's showroom for pieces of industrial furnishings and objects from the early 20th century is appropriately removed from the Drouot neighbourhood, since his own métier is so unlike anything else. Oversized light fixtures, metal bookcases, balloon moulds from the national meteorological service, all are given pride of place by the farmer turned furniture-maker and antiques dealer. Oudin claims to specialize in curiosities, and curious they may be, but his stock is presented in such a clean, elegant, modern space that he really does make industry seem a lot like art.

DESIGNER LAMPS AND FASHION
16 Heaven
83, rue des Martyrs

In the truly holistic art experience of Montmartre, this popular boutique is a marriage of designers in more ways than one. Lea-Anne Wallis is the creator of men's and women's clothes, while Jean-Christophe Peyrieux is responsible for the feather-adorned lamps and chandeliers featuring sprays of thin wires tipped with bright red balls, a cross between floral and space-age. Wallis's designs range from bold retroprints on double-vested coats to blousy trousers, bright, cummerbund-waist skirts and smooth-fitting T-shirts. Everything has a lean elegance about it, with splashes of colour ensuring it's never too serious.

BAGS OF STYLE
17 Emmanuelle Zysman
81, rue des Martyrs

Emmanuelle Zysman's first career was teaching literature, but now her bags are sold in department stores around the world. This, however, is her only shop, where she also sells clothing mainly by French designers. She says she is inspired by 'the music-hall of the 1930s, as well as contemporary photographs and flea market objects'. Her first collection in 1996 featured a variety of fabrics covered in clear vinyl. In 2002 her 'poetic universe of images' was dominated by colonialism and circus animals. Pieces in leather, embroidery, velvet and straw all please the eye and touch.

ARTY BAR
18 La Fourmi
74, rue des Martyrs

Just over the border from the 9th, La Fourmi is a bar oozing with bohemian characters who come to drink beneath its wine-bottle chandelier before heading off to neighbourhood gigs. From heavily pierced goths in white face paint and black gear to flannel-shirted loungers whose tastes are probably more of the metal variety, the crowd at La Fourmi is a good cross-section of clubbers, night owls and casual drinkers who come to peruse the event bills posted on the windows or just soak up the atmosphere of the Pigalle-Montmartre border. During the day it's a casual café where people come for a coffee, a snack and to read the paper.

CONCRETE WONDER
19 Eglise St-Jean-de-Montmartre
19, rue des Abbesses

The place des Abbesses is a picturesque spot not only for its Hector Guimard Métro entrance but also for its pioneering *fin-de-siècle* church, completed in 1904 to a design by Anatole de Baudot, former assistant to architectural visionary Eugène-Emmanuel Viollet-le-Duc, and one of the first examples in Europe of reinforced concrete used for its sculptural qualities – a thrilling and innovative reinterpretation of the Gothic vault.

HANDPAINTED TEXTILES
20 Amaya Eguizabal
45, rue Lépic

Following the rue Durantin off rue des Abbesses, the neighbourhood becomes quieter, the crowd thins out and the shops become more discreet and specialized. If you continue on the Durantin and turn left at Lépic you'll find the tiny haven of hand-painted and -dyed scarves, belts and bags by Amaya Eguizabal. Designs are delicate and finely executed by the soft-spoken Eguizabal in her mini workshop behind the doll-house-scale shop space. Eguizabal, whose designs are reasonably priced and all beautiful enough to hang on your wall, is often on her own and happy to discuss her various pieces as well as offer you a violet sweet.

BEAUTIFUL BOTTLES
21 Belle de Jour
164

THEATRE DE L'ATELIER

STOP AND STARE

22 Place Charles Dullin

- Théâtre de l'Atelier, 1, place Charles-Dullin
- Michèle Bonny, 6, place Charles-Dullin
- Jérémie Barthod, 7, rue des Trois-Frères
- Kazana, 3, rue Tardieu

If you're feeling in need of a rest from walking around the many shops of the rue d'Orsel, the place Charles-Dullin is the perfect stop. The peaceful and well-kept square around the pretty Théâtre de l'Atelier is shady and offers a lovely view of the shops along the rue des Trois-Frères, such as Jérémie Barthod bijoux, and, in the other direction, Michèle Bonny, whose hats have a frilly, flowery, far-out appeal. The march of charming boutiques continues along the rue Tardieu with bright yellow Kazana offering an abundance of scarves from modest, ethnic-patterned cottons to finely woven creations. This a neighbourhood teeming with creative flair, all within an easy strolling distance. The theatre itself was first opened in 1822 as the Théâtre Montmartre in what was the village of Orsel. In 1922 a young comedian, Charles Dullin, restarted the theatre and brought it acclaim between the wars. Today it is a reliable venue for modern drama featuring work by David Leveaux, Frédéric Bélier-Garcia and Jacques Lassalle as well as a host of international playwrights.

CREATIVE SIDE STREET

23 rue d'Orsel

- Zelia sur la Terre comme au Ciel Boutique, no. 47 ter
- Galerie Christine Diegoni, no. 47 ter
- Erbalunga, no. 47 bis
- David Emery Creation, no. 52

At the top of the rue des Martyrs, the rue d'Orsel runs east opposite the rue des Abbesses and is full of delightful boutiques. The first shop to catch your eye will probably be Zelia sur la Terre comme au Ciel, bursting with drama in silk, organza and lace. It's not your average wedding shop; Zelia creates extravagant fabric concoctions that run from medieval princess to saucy peasant and just about everything else. The Galerie Christine Diegoni fills two elegant shop spaces full of high-design furniture and objects from the 1930s to the present. Look for Pierre Paulin, Jean Prouvé and George Nelson. Farther down at Erbalunga, delicate hand-made jewelry is created in-house. Across the little road the bright lighting fixtures of David Emery Creation call out. Emery's candelabra lamps with arms of crushed velvet hung with crystals combine elements of sculpture and soft furnishings and are enough to make you want to change your wiring.

**24 FuturWare Lab
Tatiana Lebedev**
2, rue Piémontési

Russian designer Tatiana Lebedev moved to Paris in 1990 and set up her own label in 1997. Her taste is 'architectural, inspired by the Russian Constructivist style of the early 20th century'. Yet, by employing soft fabrics like cashmere, flannel and silk in warm colours, she makes architecture not only wearable but highly desirable. Sharply angled and smooth-fitting т-shirts and crisp denim skirts as well as similar lines in leather or grey felt have a definite futuristic look, but appear sensual rather than silly. As the name implies, she is also a purveyor of new technologies, so expect some unusual new materials as well as innovative cuts and combinations.

25 Fanche et Flo
19, rue Durantin

Fanche and Flo are design partners who have been pushing the boundaries of fashion since they met 13 years ago after studying at the Sorbonne. Their clothing features bold combinations of colour, pattern and texture: a т-shirt with a bright square of fabric and zip across the front, swatches of neon or contrasts of stripey knits. Recently, with partners Eric de Gesincourt, Julia Kerjean and Xavier Dumont, they have formed Sirop de Paris, designing avant-garde textiles, lighting, objects, jewelry and furnishings, and making their sole little shop in Montmartre a bright and varied beacon of creativity. Recent 'fetish' items include the 'Barbie skirt', the 'sock-pot', the 'minimal bag' and the 'bookshop flowerpot'. See for yourself.

CLASSY KIDS
26 Gaspard de la Butte
10 bis, rue Yvonne-Le-Tac

The mohair skirts, soft flannel caps and coats and chunky graphic cardigans would be at home on the big catwalk but in Catherine Malaure's atelier-shop it's the mouse, Gaspard, and his friends who get to show them off. Her designs for children from birth to age six are as clever and beautifully imaginative as they are well-made. With a boundless supply of new ideas, sometimes resulting in as many as 40 new designs in a season, Malaure claims that she never gets bored, and it's easy to see why. Here, a mere matched set of plaid trousers and hat or a textured pullover just might make you want to have children.

BOLD AND BEAUTIFUL
27 Patricia Louisor
16, rue Houdon

On a street known mainly for the fashion of its local transvestites, young, talented Patricia Louisor set up her small, vividly wrapped shop in 1991 making use of the vast fabric emporium of the nearby Marché St-Pierre to create her designs of 'simplicity and originality'. Her well-priced clothes 'for working, dancing or seduction' soon brought her notoriety, mainly by word of mouth. Today she is a featured designer among the artisans of Montmartre with a collection that is sexy with substance. Using plush fabrics cut on the bias, wrapped close to the body and flared at the wrist or ankle, she aims to create comfort of movement 'without sacrificing femininity and without adhering to the dictates of the latest fashion'.

DESIGN BY THE BOOK
28 Pages 50/70: Olivier Verlet
15, rue Yvonne-le-Tac

Opposite Gaspard de la Butte (see p. 73), the grown-up pursuit of collecting is encouraged at Olivier Verlet's Pages 50/70, which specializes in modern glass, ceramic and lighting design. There are many retro shops in Paris but Pages 50/70 continues to come top of the class (the page numbers refer to those in a book on the history of design that deal with the modern period). Along with ceramics by Jacques Ruelland, Pol Cambost and Georges Jouve are furniture and other pieces by Pierre Guariche, Pierre Paulin and Mathieu Matégot.

PINK LADIES
29 Doly'doll
41, rue des Abbesses

Hot-pink, leather-studded dressing-room doors, fuchsia, leopard-print carpet and gilded furniture welcome you to Doly'doll, a pop boutique with an interior more like a cabaret singer's boudoir. It's hard not be drawn in and overwhelmed by the décor but the clothes are worth a look too. Doly'doll has its own range of lacey appliquéd and pretty-funky shirts and skirts but carries Diesel and a few other street labels as well. It's a hotchpotch indeed but gets high marks for presentation.

DOWN-TO-EARTH CAFÉ
30 Chez Camille
8, rue Ravignan

Yellow seems to be a favoured colour for funky Parisian cafés and Chez Camille has certainly had the yellow treatment, which makes it feel all the more relaxed and welcoming. So, too, do the chess and backgammon boards and the Scrabble games. Chez Camille is a calming slice of bohemia. If the games don't grab you, you can enjoy the elevated view, then walk through the place Emile Goudeau, a lovely square, home to a number of Montmartre artists over the years, including one Pablo Picasso.

ETHNIC UNDERGROUND
31 Doudingue Bar-Restaurant
24, rue Durantin

Doudingue stands out among the drinking spots of Montmartre for its distinctive interior, derived from 'a mix of Baroque and Oriental, Parisian flea market and objects from India and Iran'. Opened by owner-manager Afshin Assadian with his wife, Valérie, and friend Jimmy Fofana in the summer of 2002, Doudingue, which means 'crazy but nice', was the trio's attempt to move from large club venues to the more intimate atmosphere of a bar and restaurant. They still have DJs spinning records but the plush bar area is good for a relaxed glass of wine or a tropical drink following an afternoon of Montmartre shopping.

OLD-FASHIONED COOKING
32 Ginette de la Côte d'Azur
101, rue Caulaincourt

Ginette must have looked exactly like this back in the 1930s: same terrace, the same lighting, tiling, mirrors and mosaics. What has surely changed, however, is the ambience, nowadays more casual-chic than hard-working. For this is one of Montmartre's bohemian bourgeois centres, chronically overcrowded, especially when the sun comes out. A few visitors have discovered the place, so do as they do: book a table, sit back and relax, sip your coffee and watch the world go by. As far as food goes, stick to the bistro basics.

HIGH-STYLE BRASSERIE
33 Le Soleil (Saint-Ouen)
109, avenue Michelet

One thing you should know before you get inside: it may look like a bistro, but it definitely isn't. Run by a former 'food hunter' who worked for some three-star chefs, seeking out the best products all around the country, Le Soleil is an upper-class brasserie, chic and cosy, offering quite simple food extremely well prepared (simplicity may sometimes be very luxurious). Try the green bean salad, any fresh fish (the owner loves seafood), roasted pigeon, the 350-gram entrecôte steak with a red wine sauce or the huge rum baba (don't even try to eat it on your own). The message is that the best products often make the best cooking.

FLEA-MARKET MECCA
34 Les Puces de Saint-Ouen
Saint-Ouen

You'll need to get there by train, as it's north of the Métro lines, but if antiques are what you're after, then it really won't do to miss this all-in-one Parisian bargain hunter's paradise. But it's not only antiques that fill the large markets here: there is a vast selection, from art galleries and rare-book dealers to reproduction furniture.

Cassolette de Girolles

Saumon d'Ecosse en

Tomates Mozzarella

Carpaccio de Thon à

Gaspacho Andalou

Salade de queues de lan

Melon de Cavaillon au

Pavé de Lotte rôhe et

PASTIS
51

COGNAC

Beaubourg
Marais
Canal St-Martin

Whatever your opinion of the high-tech nakedness of the Centre Pompidou, there is no escaping its role as an inspiration and symbol of new design, as the shops and galleries in the surrounding Beaubourg neighbourhood have demonstrated since the building's completion in the 1970s. Going east into the Marais, literally 'the swamp', the Musée Carnavalet and the elegant Place des Vosges signal another era entirely, as do the many lovely 16th- and 17th-century *hôtels particuliers* that were built to house personalities almost as grand as the architecture. The Marais also has historic associations with craftspeople, a reputation that has been given a recent polish, as young Parisian and international couturiers, artisans and design specialists congregate in areas like the rue Vieille-du-Temple and the small but finely tuned atelier-galleries around its northern end and on the rue Debelleyme. The rue Charlot, still comparatively undiscovered and undeveloped, is home to some of the area's most innovative designers ('developed' here meaning not a new building full of name brands but an old residential or industrial building being spruced up and inhabited by one or two designers or a small cooperative whose talents are not yet matched by their turnover). On the rue du Roi-de-Sicile and rue des Rosiers you will find fashion boutiques with as much originality as the big names on the Left Bank but with premises (and prices) that are decidedly less opulent. Throughout the creative density of the 3rd and 4th arrondissements are bookshops, exhibition spaces and bars tucked between and around the historic sites. Aided and abetted by a spirited gay population, this is also home to some of the liveliest café culture in Paris, with old favourites and trendy hotspots filling out a night-time destination for those seeking contemporary style tinged with the romance of historic architecture.

The hive of creativity has been spreading steadily northwards to the latest of Paris's rejuvenated areas, the hip, bohemian and village-like Canal St-Martin in the 10th arrondissement. Perhaps this is because lower rents have lured designers, architects and media start-ups in the area; or perhaps it's because the trains from London decant their international visitors hourly at the Gare du Nord a few blocks away. No matter — a visit to the shops and groovy cafés of the canal area, especially after spending time around the tourist hubs, is like travelling to a rural French town (especially when the quai de Valmy is closed for pedestrians) with urban sophistication. Drinking or dining canalside today is calmer, cooler, less frenetic and showy than the Left Bank or even the Marais. It's a place where the aesthetic dynamism of Paris feels accessible and personable in a way it must have once done before the tour buses and chain stores moved in.

1 Centre Pompidou
place Georges Pompidou

Some people find it amusing that a conservative politician like Georges Pompidou fostered such avant-garde architectural projects as this extraordinary work by Richard Rogers and Renzo Piano. As striking as it is today, it certainly caused a few jaws to drop when it was opened in 1977, with its exposed servicing pipes and framework jutting up from the old Beaubourg neighbourhood. But the building, with its contemporary art galleries, has lived to be loved and a revamp in 2000, which included the addition of a rooftop restaurant (see below), has given a new lease of life.

DESIGN LINES
2 Le Domicile
25, rue du Renard

This design furniture shop is the genuine article. Three designers, Christophe Pillet, Jean-Marie Massaud and Dominique Mathieu, make their limited-edition furniture, lighting and objects for Maryline Brustolin and her sister, Corrine, who opened this gallery, designed by architect Gilles Deseudavy, in 2001. The shop is unique in Paris, Maryline says, in that it carries high-design furnishings for every aspect of the home, from flooring and rugs to door handles, sofas, chairs and lighting. In addition to the clean-lined pieces by their in-house designers there is work from the Dutch collective Droog, lighting by Philippe Starck, ceramics by Marcel Wanders and amazing sponge furniture by Massayo Ave.

AN EVEN NEWER TWIST
3 Georges
Centre Pompidou, place Georges Pompidou

This is another piece of the Costes brothers' empire, on the sixth floor of the Pompidou, with breathtaking views over the city's rooftops, probably the best view you can get from a restaurant anywhere in the city. Most interesting is the unusual architecture, designed by Brendan MacFarlane and Dominique Jakob (see also p. 86), a strange mixture of space-age influences and hollowed-out organic shapes, alternating with icy aluminium and splashes of colour – cold and shiny on the outside, warm and inviting inside.

ZEN-LIKE APPEARANCE
4 Bô
8, rue St-Merri

Bô is a spot of beauty, named for the tree under which Buddha received inspiration. Objects and accessories by French and international designers are displayed in a modern setting: crackle-glazed tableware made by Pierre Cazenove for the centuries-old French manufacturer JARS, as well as his vases; furniture, sculpture and Japanese-inspired ceramics by Gilles Caffier; a Karim Rashid candelabra and metalwork vases and objects by Michael Aram. Stunning wall lamps, or 'tableaux illuminés', by Catherine Grandidier also stand out. Andie Vandevoorde's glowing red rice-paper wall-panel lamp is a favourite.

ARCHITECTURE AND ART
5 La Galerie d'Architecture
11, rue des Blancs-Manteaux

Architects Gian Mauro Maurizio and Olga Pugliese set up their intimate modern white space on the rue des Blancs-Manteaux 'to show the work of contemporary architects in an alternative space, to show what is going on now with architecture and to show the work of young architects as well as the more famous'. Opened in 1999, the gallery focuses on Europe, but they have also exhibited work from Japan and the U.S. A small café and bookshop make this a great, friendly place for a quick architecture injection.

FEMININE FEELING
6 Azzedine Alaïa
7, rue de Moussy

Confronted with the blank façade on the rue de Moussy, don't be put off. Ring the bell and enter the world of Tunisian-born designer Azzedine Alaïa, whose long, lean, figure-hugging designs have won him a clientele of models and celebrities eager to show off their perfect form in some of his. 'Sexy' doesn't begin to describe them, as some dresses on mannequins look as if they've been poured into a tall, curvy mould, but, clingy and contoured as his pieces are, they are also made of fine fabrics, delicately patterned knits, kid-like leather, crepe or thick cotton weave, and they all have that combination of design and quality that make them hard to resist even with their high-profile price tags. The shop itself is a wonder, a former factory turned echoing showroom, atelier and gallery for the work of Alaïa's friend, artist Julian Schnabel, who also helped transform the brick-lined space into a spare, modern fashion statement.

THE HAMMAM TREATMENT
7 Les Bains du Marais
31–33, rue des Blancs-Manteaux

DRINKS ON THE SQUARE
8 Café Beaubourg
43, rue St-Merri

At the risk of employing a much-used term, the Marais baths really are an oasis in the city. Not just the services, of which there are many, but immediately in the entrance, where warm wood and cool tile, plants and spicy aromas greet visitors. There is a salon at left and a bank of wood and glass cabinets full of impeccable rows of beauty and skincare products at right. Straight ahead is a little café where clients can have a snack, a drink or a health-enhancing meal. In the Bains du Marais, you can have your hair cut and/or coloured, you can be manicured, pedicured or waxed, have a purifying facial or sauna or hammam treatment and a variety of massages with or without essential oils. The baths are open to women Monday through Wednesday and to men Thursday through Saturday. Weekends are mixed, so clients must wear bathing suits.

An early Costes production, the Café Beaubourg was designed by one of France's most celebrated architects, Christian de Portzamparc. Its red, black, cream and white cushioned outdoor seating continues to stand out from the average rattan-wrapped bistro chair, despite a little wear. Outdoor tables on the plaza of the Centre Pompidou are a popular lounging spot but fill up surprisingly quickly with people tippling wine or one of the cocktails from a list that includes a Bronx Bomber *and* a Cape Codder. Indoors, a galleried two-level space is dramatized by bookcases, dark-leather-upholstered furniture and a catwalk. The menu is fairly traditional French but graciously makes a nod to the States with a hamburger. To beat the crowds, get there before noon and enjoy one of several breakfast dishes while gazing at the activity around the Pompidou.

LEATHER LOVES

9 Serge Amoruso

39, rue du Roi-de-Sicile

If you are someone who truly appreciates *haute maroquinerie* then you should stop by Serge Amoruso, not just to see the fine leather goods, but to watch the craftsmen at work, cutting, stitching, stamping, all by hand, all right there in the shop. Amoruso calls himself a 'tanner and saddler but above all a creative designer'. It is the combination of those things that gives his products the quality of the artisan rather than just the trend-setter, although he is also the latter: check out the vanity case on brushed steel legs or the post-box-style cigar pot.

ÉLÉGANCE SUPRÊME

10 L'Ambroisie

138

BURGUNDIAN CHARMS

11 Le Bourguignon du Marais

52, rue François-Miron

Would you sell your soul to the devil for Pinot Noir and Chardonnay? Then you'll probably be glad to learn that this fancy bistro has a cellarful of upper-class Burgundy wines, and not necessarily expensive ones, which is quite unusual. If you're not sure what to choose, ask owner Jacques Bavard (whose name means 'talkative'): he'll be sure to have a secret bottle that'll go well with Burgundian snails, a large slice of *jambon persillé*, *œufs en meurette* (traditional poached eggs in a red wine sauce) or *andouillette* (chitterling sausage) from the famous producer Duval. Some might call that heaven.

CONTEMPORARY CLASSICS

12 Sentou Galerie

163

13 Martin Grant
32, rue des Rosiers

The lettering above still says COIFFURE, from the days when this was a barber-shop, but now the pale blue frontage is home to designs by the young Australian Martin Grant, who has a little workshop in the back behind the curtain. The arrangement is expectedly spare with only a few rails showing his carefully crafted pieces, but they sing out with style. Grant has a penchant for darts, high up all along the waist and even at the elbows. His needlecord jackets, all with matching trousers, feature narrow, accordion-style pleats running vertically to further tailor the heavy fabric to the body. Similarly his 'Priest Coat', in angora, wool or calfskin, is tightened up with darted waist and arms. It all makes for a smart, crisp, very tailored look. Blouses are lighter-weight and brighter, but the four-button cuff and substantial collar mean that 'blousy' is somebody else's idea of fashion.

14 Kyungmee J.
38, rue du Roi-de-Sicile

Kyungmee is a talented young Korean-American designer who, after studying at the Fashion Institute of Technology in New York, came to Paris six years ago as a tourist and never went back. Her small atelier is the sole outlet for her designs, which reflect a truly original eye. Some might see the Asian inspiration in her delicate floral patterns or in some of the square-cut tops, but Kyungmee says her ideas are all her own. 'I try not to see too much of what other people do,' she says. 'Every season is like a blank page.' Except that she continues to evolve some of her favourite themes, like the solid wool coat or skirt with the 'cascade' of contrasting fabric at the front. A lot of her clients are regulars, she says, and people of similar persuasion, 'architects, artists, dancers', who are probably attracted to the elegant asymmetry, the imaginative combinations of colour and pattern and the quality craft.

15 Café du Trésor
7–9, rue du Trésor

On the strangely quiet pedestrianized rue du Trésor – almost everyone wants to be on the rue Vieille-du-Temple, no matter how crowded – restaurateur Laurent Taïeb (see also p. 36) opened the Café du Trésor. Beneath gaudy gold-and-black awnings are an array of rooms decorated in a sort of futuristic Baroque: all one colour, walls, ceilings, plasterwork decoration, with matching Venetian-style glass chandeliers. The first set of rooms is white, the next frame of the picture is red – chairs, tables, walls – with chartreuse in the room behind, then you get to the most intimate, the blue room. Italian-inspired snacks are served but this is primarily a nocturnal drinking spot – young, trendy, happening and lots of room for mingling. Other attractions include a downstairs massage room and live goldfish swimming in the vetrines above the toilets.

16 Cloître des Billettes
24, rue des Archives

Next to the great red doors that mark the Lutheran Church, the cloisters, which are medieval and predate the church by about 300 years, have been given over to the exhibition of work by new and emerging artists. The work of the artists – the exhibitions change twice a month – hangs in the peaceful shelter of the colonnaded Gothic courtyard, the worn ancient stone making a spare but spirited backdrop for the contemporary art and ethnic objects that are displayed there. The exhibitions are usually free and the cloisters themselves are worth a peaceful look.

17 Papier+
9, rue du Pont Louis-Philippe

In 1976 Laurent Tisné left the world of publishing to open a shop selling blank books. That is to say, he sold high-quality, cloth-covered books with sewn bindings and pages of sturdy paper. Today the shop run by his British wife, Elizabeth Wrightson, is still one of the best sources for traditionally made blank books in an assortment of colours. Notebooks of varying sizes, address books and their ever-popular photograph albums (with thick pages and not a hint of cellophane) are filled with laid and woven papers, from Swedish Ingres to French Balkiss to English Conqueror. There are also stationery sets, sketch-books and blotters as well as loose-leaf paper, envelopes and card.

18 Hôtel du Bourg Tibourg
122

THE ART OF BOOKS
19 Florence Loewy
9–11, rue de Thorigny

Where better to demonstrate the beauty and utility of architecture than in an architecture and art bookshop? At Florence Loewy architects Dominique Jakob and Brendan MacFarlane, whose modular interventions are in evidence at the Georges restaurant (see p. 81), took an architects' favoured material, birch-ply, and created curving compartmental towers to accommodate the wide range of books in a relatively small Parisian shop space. Look carefully and you can see the books stored ingeniously behind the other books. The stock itself is a wide range of volumes in many languages on contemporary and late-20th-century art, architecture, design and graphics. There is also a small exhibition space.

PARLOUR GAMES
20 L'Apparemment
18, rue des Coutures-St-Gervais

In Paris there are cafés that combine wine and car culture, wine and film, wine and fetishes of the Virgin Mary (see p. 108) and here we have wine and games ('apparently', hence the name). In these cosy, wood-panelled rooms just opposite the Picasso Museum and among the many arty boutiques and galleries of the Marais you can take a culture break of sorts, order a glass or bottle and settle into a leather armchair for a quick game of cards or challenge someone to one of several board games.

DISCOUNT DESIGNER WEAR
21 L'Habilleur
44, rue de Poitou

If you always thought that the latest prêt-à-porter designs were beyond your bank account but coveted them nonetheless, then you'll be pleased to happen upon this small bounty of a discount shop. The selection is dominated by women's wear but there are men's clothes as well, from such big fashion names as Paul et Joe, John Richmond and Plein Sud, also things by Vivienne Westwood and Patrick Cox at around half price. The collections follow the same fashion-season cycle but one year later, so these are all ever so slightly dated but no less striking.

The revolutionary fanatic Robespierre lived for a while at no. 64, but the little rue de Poitou is now making history of a different sort. Since around the year 2000 designers and gallerists have moved into the area, overflowing from the gallery haven of the rue Vieille-du-Temple. Now you can find luxury bedlinens and home accessories at Passage, artful textiles at Florence Dufieux and innovative handbags at Karine Dupont.

The houses on this street date from the 13th century, so the recent upsurge of galleries, boutiques, bars and restaurants only adds to its medieval charm. From tapestries and tea shops to furnishings and fine linens, there is almost no luxury item that you cannot find here. The Belle Hortense 'bar littéraire', sets the tone, with a heady mix of wine and books, with bottles of Côtes du Rhône and Châteauneuf du Pape sharing window space with books by Paul Celan and Martin Broda and literary postcards featuring the likes of Beckett, Marx and Proust alongside their more memorable quotes. Inside are more literary books for sale and a bar where you can contemplate the beauty of the written word. Once the head of an English fashion house, José Lévy began his own label with a shop in the 11th arrondissement and moved to the Marais, selling mostly menswear: Lévy made v-neck sweaters a fashion statement when he made the v longer and leaner and the knit that bit finer in solid colours woven with subtle hints of contrast. A few of the funkier pieces sport appliquéd stars, and men's wool duffle coats in pink and light blue might take some getting used to.

The rue Vieille-du-Temple is chock-a-block with art and design galleries but there are a few must-sees. Christophe Delcourt is a self-taught young furniture designer whose dedication to craftsmanship (à la Frank Lloyd Wright and Pierre Chareau, among others) has won him acclaim among French design enthusiasts. His gallery is full of his smooth, simple pieces in oak and walnut with quirky details. He recommends the nearby Galerie Pierre, a well-known shop and exhibition space for fine ceramics, in stoneware, earthenware and porcelain. Mars is a funkier, unmarked gallery and shop space painted khaki green for the recycled army canvas that partner Yves Andrieux uses for bags lined with perky red floral print and other pieces. Vincent Jalbert makes the rough-hewn wood furniture and the ingenious latex-felt garden pots.

This stylish eatery, where organic meets high design, is 'fun and healthy'. Cool green tones recall the many specialty teas on the menu, which include a selection to induce 'bien dormir' that goes much further than your average chamomile, and a special mix called 'Love Suprême' made from a concoction of cinnamon, cardamom leaves and flower petals that is almost too beautiful to steep. There are cordials and cakes and a menu that emphasizes light dishes centred on vegetables and cereals, which can all be prepared for take-away. The striking interiors with lacquered concrete floor, steel and cool green box elements are the work of Philippe de Méo, who has worked with Moët & Chandon, Parfums Jean Paul Gaultier and Baron Philippe de Rothschild and is ubiquitous on the rue Charlot, with his design agency at no. 58 and his shop, Resodiversion, at no. 43. If you hurry you may still be able to pick up some of those wonderful moulded green plastic chairs.

If you are one of those people who get a shiver down your spine reading a copy of a 1960s *Vogue*, the Archives de la Presse just might be your idea of heaven. A treasure trove for art directors and fashionistas looking for ideas, the store specializes in vintage publications of sports, fashion, cinema, travel and cookery as well as storing miles of old newspapers. There are hundreds of back issues of *Vogue*, *Marie Claire* and *Paris Match*, including a special collection dedicated to magazines featuring Princess Diana since her first press appearance. The staff are indispensable and, they say, 'very organized'.

Like the extravagant Musée Jacquemart André (p. 62), the smaller and more intimate Cognacq-Jay is the result of a significant private collection donated by individuals – Ernest Cognacq and his wife, Louise Jay – to the city of Paris. Cognacq founded the Samaritaine department store, which he built up from a small shop on the Pont Neuf to one of the city's grandest department stores, opened in 1900. Cognacq used his increasing fortune to buy art, antiques and decorative objects that now adorn the 16th-century Hôtel Donan, which was refurbished to provide a setting for the amazing collection of largely 18th-century art and furnishings. Entire suites of furniture are arranged with complementary period boiserie, carpets and paintings.

Madame de Sévigné, the famed 18th-century literary lady, was one of the early occupants of the newly built Marais mansions. Now the rue de Sévigné continues the enhancement of culture. Notable stops include the fashion photography bookshop Comptoir de l'Image, opened by a former assistant to Richard Avedon. More artistic endeavour is on display at the contemporary Galerie Chez Valentin; head for the north end of the rue and the worn blue doors, one of which is usually open. The glassed-in space might be entirely covered in zig-zag lines of black electrical tape, or it might have a plain old contemporary art exhibition inside.

32 La Marine

55 bis, quai de Valmy

It's often packed, its bright red frontage framing the reassuringly worn interiors and its prime site along the canal making it immediately attractive even to those who have never been inside. The creative, youthful atmosphere of the neighbourhood is also apparent here and it's one of those places that survives on doing the basics well (good, unpretentious dishes and reasonable drink) and letting the spirit of the crowd do the rest. In an area that is fast becoming a favourite for hip Parisians, it won't be long before places like this are all too rare.

GROOVY READ

33 Artazart

83, quai de Valmy

The graphic orange shopfront covers not just an art book store but a centre for creative endeavour. Anything between two covers that is to do with art, architecture or graphic design can be found here, as well as a host of things you wouldn't expect from a bookstore. Stop in here on a stroll along the canal to browse the latest photography and graphics books and the avant-garde design magazines in several languages, but also to visit a photographic exhibition.

PRETTY IN PINK

34 Stella Cadente

93, quai de Valmy

The mauve, pink and lilac hues give the subtle signal that this is a place focused on feminine flair. The fashion label set up by designer Stanislassia Klein has quickly become a must for savvy Parisian women and for those who just like the soft, unusual details she adds to simple, pretty designs. The former tool warehouse has been given a light, romantic lift. You'll want to touch everything, from the feather-trimmed chiffon shift dresses to the beaded bags and diaphanous shawls. And this is low-pressure selling, since you won't need much convincing as you sit in a pastel sofa draped in alluring fabrics and sip a hospitable cup of tea while considering your purchases and gazing out over the tree-shaded bridge.

FUGITIVE OENOPHILIA

35 Le Verre Volé

152

36 Chez Prune

71, quai de Valmy

On a picturesque corner of the quai de Valmy and rue Beaurepaire sits a funky cafe-bar overlooking the Canal St-Martin. The bold mustard-yellow walls, mosaic-covered tables and buzzy locals tell you that Chez Prune is not about staid café offerings. The staff are welcoming and relaxed despite the fact that Prune has proved increasingly popular as the canal area attracts an ever groovier set. A worthy stop for lunch, evening tapas or drinks until 2 am, it's a favourite among media professionals and the young and fashionable. The menu is classic French, with blood sausages among its most popular offerings, and includes a range of freshly prepared *assiettes 'faites maison'*. The wine list is extensive, but the young men behind the bar will as gladly pour you a cool *pression*.

ALL THINGS BRIGHT AND BEAUTIFUL

37 Antoine et Lili

95, quai de Valmy

Antoine et Lili's 'village' is a departure from their chain of shops in and around Paris and abroad in its collection of fashion, homeware, accessories and café in separate, candy-coloured shops. Bright does not begin to describe the combinations of red, pink, orange, yellow and turquoise that serve as the backdrop to the range of modern ethnic pieces. Vibrant patterns of pottery and linens fill the Déco shop, along with trinkets and bric-à-brac, while flower-decked umbrellas hang with beaded belts and floral and brilliant-striped T-shirts, paisley blouses and flared trousers. Refuel in style in the fuchsia 'tea-house'.

LIFE AND ART

38 Fondation Icar

159, quai de Valmy

The Fondation Icar (Institute for Cooperation of Art and Research) is the Paris base for a U.S. not-for-profit foundation that develops 'programmes in the arts, sciences, and humanities'. This space, in a former industrial building on the Canal St-Martin, was designed by Dutch artist Rens Lipsius to represent 'the ideal artist's studio'. Lipsius' design is, light, open and inviting, with the aim of making Icar's cross-disciplinary programme of events, which includes everything from exhibitions of art in all media to dramatic performances and concerts, accessible to all.

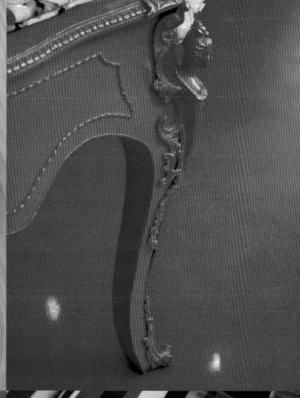

"19ᴴ-22ᴴ30" LES ASSIETTES "19ᴴ-22ᴴ30"

* **PANIER DU JARDINIER:** 7 €
Crudités, Sauce au fromage Blanc
échalotte et Ciboulette.

* **ASSIETTE 3 COULEURS:** 7 €
Tarama, Houmos, Tapenade "faits maison".

* **ASSIETTE DE FROMAGE:** 8 €
Cantal "entre deux", Crottin à l'huile
d'olive, Bleu d'Auvergne, Brie de Meaux.

* **ASSIETTE DE CHARCUTERIE:** 8 €
Tampon de Pays de chez Mas,
Saucisse Sèche, Paté.

_____

HUITRES

16 €

Antoine & Lili

39 L'Atmosphère

49, rue Lucien-Sampaix

Just up the road from the villagey shop row of Stella Cadente and Antoine et Lili, this is a favourite spot in the Canal St-Martin scene with a funky mix of fresh flowers and plants, dried bunches, old furnishings and bright crockery for those reasonably priced *pichets* of wine. Outdoor seating is on the canalside and couldn't be more atmospheric. It no longer has live music at night but does on a Sunday afternoon.

40 L'Ile Enchantée

65, boulevard de la Villette

One of the new bright spots to emerge with the resurrection of the local area, L'Ile Enchantée demonstrates that new and old can exist in a rather vibrant harmony. The interiors of this rejuvenated bar have been livened up with just enough colourful touches to emphasize a degree of youthful zeal in an establishment that has become so popular it is now difficult to get a table. Traditional attention to French cooking and a wine list handwritten across an old mirror are a nod to the more serious business of serving up good food and drink to the new bohemian Belleville/Canal St-Martin crowd it now draws.

THE TABLE LESS CROWDED

41 Chez Casimir

6, rue de Belzunce

Among the young 'neo bistro' chefs (trained by two- or three-star chefs who have decided not to open restaurants themselves) is Thierry Breton, whose restaurant next door, Chez Michel, is mostly jam-packed. Therefore, try his more casual annexe, Chez Casimir, with its neutral, old-style café non-décor and its tasty, less Britanny-influenced food. Be careful, though: this is a place where you'll need a user's manual. First course/main course or main course/dessert is the way things go here. But your mouth will water when your fish soup or your roasted chicken with peas arrives. Very affordable wine list.

ARTISAN-MADE BAGS AND SHOES

42 Jamin-Puech

169

HISTORIC TABLEWARE

43 Baccarat/Musée du Cristal

30 bis, rue de Paradis

In a city populated with museums celebrating everything from ancient history to the handheld fan, the Parisian headquarters of the famed crystal manufacturer has seen fit to celebrate its own aesthetic and technical achievements. Behind a grand façade and up two flights of wide oak stairs are shining examples of why Baccarat has been an enduring mark of French design: settings created for European royalty in 1764, a fine crystal ewer given to French King Charles X in 1828 and a pair of drippingly opulent electric candelabra made for, but never delivered to Nicholas II of Russia. Plain and tinted crystal tableware and strikingly modern decanters are arranged along open tables (not behind glass) and in situ where their perfection can be appreciated up close. Some contemporary pieces are available for purchase.

Bercy
Bastille
Ménilmontant
Belleville

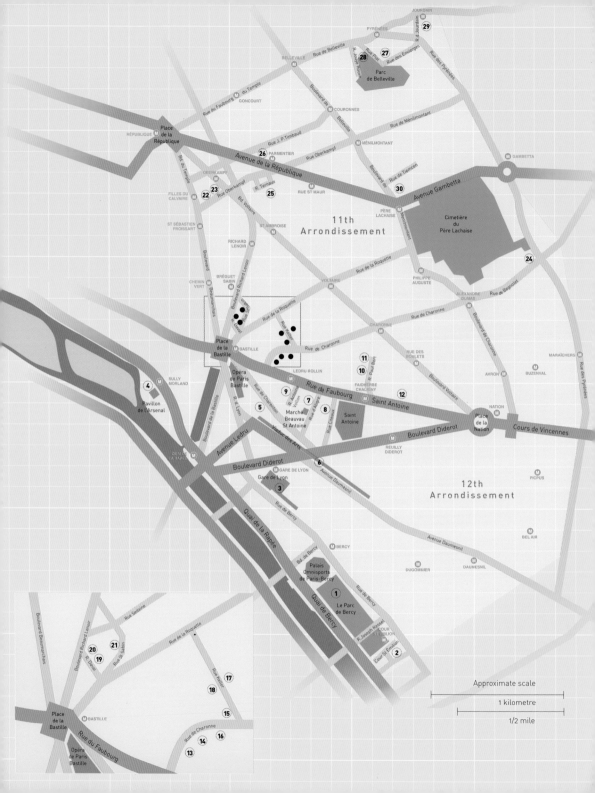

Since the French mastered the formal garden there arose the question what they would do for an encore. But evidence of their unbounded botanical inventiveness lies in the modern parks springing up around the capital, such as the Parc André Citroën (p. 36) and the thoughtful mix of geometric and romantic arrangements of the vast Parc de Bercy (p. 100). While many urban capitals are bemoaning the loss of city parks, the Parisians have developed the largest green space since Baron Haussmann boulevardized the city in the 19th century, which, together with the renovation of the former wine warehouses of the Bercy district, the construction of the large Palais Omnisports and a dedicated Métro line, has quite literally brought a breath of fresh air to an area dominated by train lines and large, inhospitable streets. It also makes a soothing introduction to the neighbourhoods to the north, which embrace urbanism in all its gritty reality.

Moving north, we encounter the avenue Daumesnil, dominated by a disused viaduct that, in a typically positive turn of regeneration, has become the home of the Viaduc des Arts (p. 103), a long varied parade of brick-arched spaces that have been restored and converted for use as modern-looking galleries and craft studios. Farther north, the Bastille beckons, with funky bars and own-design boutiques grouped around the rue de Charonne, rue Keller and the tiny rue Daval. In the early 1990s the Bastille felt the flurry of regeneration, but this wasn't about new members of the bourgeoisie buying up old neglected warehouses and renovating them so much as club promoters looking for cheap big spaces to light up and fill with techno beats and crowds of enthusiastic dance divas. The wide, imposing avenues radiating from both the place de la Bastille and the République were never going to have the sparkle of the Champs-Élysées, but they were going to have an ample supply of street cred, which hasn't been entirely lost despite its popularity with younger tourists. Restaurants and cafés range from the old workers' haunts to the new and enterprising, with some of the more stylish establishments setting up east in the neighbourhood of the Faubourg-St-Antoine and rue Paul-Bert.

The République and rue Oberkampf also sizzled with youthful zeal and edgy street style in the most recent Bastille revolution. They continue to buzz with café and night life. Shops and bars too reflect the appeal of the streetwise Paris urban scene that is well away from the mainstream tourists and the heavily commercialized districts: young designers line the rue Oberkampf and appealing bars and cafés stretch even farther from the popular fray into the arty bonhomie of Ménilmontant and Belleville.

1 Parc de Bercy

It's only a few stops from the centre of town on the Métro but it's a world away in terms of atmosphere. The Parc de Bercy was completed in 1997 and resulted from the redevelopment of an area dominated by old wine warehouses, a depot for the produce that was shipped to Paris by river. The development was an ambitious project, the largest park created since the reorganization by Haussmann in the 19th century. It included the construction of the large, turf-covered Palais Omnisports de Paris-Bercy overlooking the modern landscaped Jardin de la Mémoire (garden of memory), which is actually a number of differently arranged green spaces that incorporate old rail lines and stone paths as well as the existing centuries-old trees. In the tradition of formal French garden design made modern (see also p. 36), there are geometric arrangements incorporating canals, bridges, ponds and plantings of mature trees, flowers and shrubs into a delightful space for walking, picnicking or playing, with new and interesting landscapes around every corner.

WINE WAREHOUSE REDUX
2 Bercy Village
  • Résonances, 9, cour St-Émilion
  • Chai 33, 33, cour St-Émilion

The actual wine stores of Bercy have had a facelift along with the warehouse district. Cour St-Émilion, at its heart, has its own Métro stop just after Bercy park and has recently been converted into an upscale shopping parade along a cobblestoned lane. Everything looks bright and shiny here but large black-and-white photographs along the various passages show the area when the wine depot was active. There are cafés and restaurants where you can also have tea or coffee outside or in a high-tech-rustic interior, and shops, from arty boutiques to fine children's toys, have filled the smart-looking street. Among them is the original branch of Résonances, an upmarket do-it-yourself and home specialty shop created by François Lemarchand, founder of the extremely popular Nature et découvertes chain and responsible for Pier Import in Paris. Comparisons with Wiliams Sonoma in America and the Conran Shop in London signal the emphasis on traditional, high-quality goods, such as hardware and kitchen appliances, with a modern eye for gourmet and designer products. Four wine cellars converted by Architral into a clean-lined emporium stock everything from paintbrushes to paté. For an altogether different experience, there is the latest 'concept' bar from Thierry Bégué, the man behind

Buddha Bar and Barrio Latino. Chai 33 is a huge (1,350 square metres [13,500 square feet]) former storehouse divided into different spaces on three levels – a wine shop, a bar, a lounge, a restaurant and a bistro, not to mention a double terrace. Chai 33 tries to promote wine drinking by focusing on the taste and power of wines instead of their variety, a novel idea for the French.

NEXT STOP: BELLE ÉPOQUE

3 Le Train Bleu

place Louis Armand, Gare de Lyon

It's hard to believe, but this gorgeous Belle Époque interior with its gilt mirrors, wall paintings and medallions was for many years a rather mediocre café with a nice design. Created for the 1900 Exhibition and named after the line that used to connect Paris with Lyon and Marseille, the restaurant is a listed monument and now the cuisine has been uplifted by chef André Signoret to better match the heights of decorative fancy. A red carpet runs through an enfilade of Baroque revival rooms where booths in carved wood sit against painted woodwork, mythical figures peer down from grand arches and chandeliers blaze while diners enjoy classic French dishes and those at the bar sink into the leather Chesterfield sofas and feast on the spectacle.

MODEL DEVELOPMENT

4 Pavillon de l'Arsenal

21, boulevard Morland

Opened in 1998 in an old department store warehouse, the Pavillon de l'Arsenal chronicles the architectural and urban history of Paris. Large-scale photographs of buildings past and present with descriptions of the works of various architects fill the walls, while scale models of the city, one of 40 square metres, afford a bird's-eye view. A recent addition by one of the city's most high-profile young designers, Christian Biecher, is the video lounge, where red neon draws you towards a corner of individual curved polycarbonate enclosures (illuminated in red), in which you can choose from 120 films on the work of different architects in the city and listen on your own headphones. The group video lounge is next door, where a bank of screens play a film about the city. Ongoing temporary exhibitions staged by the current big names in architecture are dynamic and informative. And it's free.

LATE-NIGHT CLUB CHIC

5 Le China Club

158

CREATIVE CAVERNS

6 Viaduc des Arts

Avenue Daumesnil
- Créations Chérif, no. 13
- Maison Fey, no. 15
- Malhia, no. 19
- VIA, nos 29–33
- Le Viaduc Café, no. 43
- Vertical, no. 63
- Cyrille Varet, no. 67
- Marie Lavande, no. 83

The arches of a disused railway viaduct have been cleaned up and glassed in and now house a parade of craft shops and ateliers. Tapestries, furnishings and lighting are prominent as are gallery spaces and exposition/showrooms. Some good stops are Créations Chérif, featuring velvet purple, orange and red curvy sofas and chairs. Maison Fey does leather-covered, stamped and embossed books, frames and furnishings; Malhia overflows with gorgeous fabrics woven on-site and in full view and available as sweaters, scarves, coats and shawls. Buy one of their reasonably priced pieces and come away with a hand-decorated Malhia bag. VIA (Valorisation de l'Innovation dans l'Ameublement), which promotes communication between designers and manufacturers, has offices and a permanent exhibition of furniture, textiles and home accessories. Le Viaduc Café has lots of pavement tables and jazz brunches on Sundays. Vertical features sculptural wood and vegetation, while no. 67 houses the wild nouveau Baroque designs of Cyrille Varet, who produces curving brushed steel in asymmetrical shapes and upholsters it in jewel tones. Marie Lavande specializes in the conservation of fine linens using soap flakes, lavender oil and rice starch. You can watch the white-coated women hand-stitching and ironing who are experts in the 17th-century technique of 'breaking and folding' table linens.

SECOND-HAND FINDS

7 Marché d'Aligre

place d'Aligre

If the Viaduc des Arts leaves you wishing for something a little more rough and ready, then a short walk around behind the viaduct will be worth your while. A small collection of traders has been gathering in the place d'Aligre since it was donated by nuns from the abbey of Saint Antoine before the French Revolution. This is one of those places rumoured to be on the list of more serious dealers looking for a real 'find'.

WORKERS' CHIC

8 L'Ebauchoir

43–45, rue de Cîteaux

There was a time when Paris had hundreds of places like this, mostly dedicated to a working-class clientele, since their prices were cheaper than cheap. Things have changed, obviously, but one can still sense that special atmosphere in this highly arty joint in the upper Bastille area, where the hip and the hard-working get along pretty well. Try the place at lunchtime and you'll see what the neighbourhood must have been like 50 years ago. Leeks vinaigrette, marinated herrings with potatoes, veal liver in a honey sauce and the monumental hard-boiled egg with mayonnaise will be part of your trip back in time.

DIET BUSTERS

9 Le Square Trousseau

1, rue Antoine-Vollon

Since some fashionable designers have invaded the Bastille neighbourhood (Jean Paul Gaultier, for instance, had his headquarters near by), this sublime Belle Époque bistro has become a high-profile celeb spot, where supermodels have been spotted ditching their diets for some home-made foie gras. Other nice choices are the baby chicken roasted with mustard (less than 900 calories), the steak tartare (almost fat-free), the crispy boudin (black pudding) with apple and cinnamon or the black-cherry soup. Regulars consider some dishes are more successful than others, and they're right. But everybody agrees that the staff are cheerful and the wine list is worth the trip.

10 L'Ecailler du Bistrot

22, rue Paul-Bert

For oyster fanatics visiting Paris, don't even think of going anywhere but L'Ecailler du Bistrot, one of the best fish and oyster bistros in town, very possibly the best. During the season (the French have a saying: 'never eat oysters during the months without an 'r' in the name', that is, from May to August), you'll find a dozen species, from the classic *fine de claire* to the less well-known 'Utah Beach' from Normandy. With some great bread and butter, a glass of muscadet or quincy (fine Sauvignon), you can almost taste the sea spray.

11 Bistrot Paul Bert

18, rue Paul-Bert

Here's an appetizing and highly affordable bistro, whose impressive owner (both for his range of wines and his knowledge) will probably love to tell you about an unknown winegrower he has just met. The chef who works for him understands that his dishes simply have to get along with the wines, producing a cuisine that rejoices in the classic (lentil soup with foie gras, cassoulet with smoked Britanny *andouille*, extra-large rib steak). The décor is superb as well, creating a consciously old-fashioned atmosphere. All Paris's simple pleasures are here.

12 Chez Ramulaud

269, rue du Faubourg-St-Antoine

Since this lovely bistro opened a couple of years ago, it has scored ever-growing success. Some early fans regret that the place seems more arrogant than it used to be, as a consequence: if you've booked a table at 8.30 pm, you'd best not arrive at 8.31. But don't complain: you're here to be beguiled by one of the most intriguing bistros in Paris, run by people who are eager to cultivate conviviality. The wine list offers prices as cheap as you will find anywhere. So grab a couple of bottles: they'll help you forget any clumsy welcome.

FOR WINE LOVERS
13 Le Café du Passage

12, rue de Charonne

Paris should have dozens of bars like this one, especially for true wine lovers who like laid-back atmospheres – if that sounds like you, this place will surely become one of your favourites. Situated near the Bastille, the Café du Passage offers more than 300 different wines, most of them from the so-called 'new vineyards' (Rhône valley, Languedoc-Roussillon, Loire valley), boasting great vintages, reasonably priced. Food is not forgotten: nice plates of fine charcuteries, a classic but perfectly tasty steak tartare or some well-cooked pasta.

RELAXED CHIC
14 Isabel Marant

168

A PLACE TO PAUSE
15 Pause Café

41, rue de Charonne

The jolly-looking corner cafe on the junction of rue Keller is a good place to stop any time – and that is this otherwise straightforward café's great virtue. A wide outdoor seating area affords a nice view of the converging streets and people. The old bistro has been updated with light wood chairs, warm mustard walls and repainted ornamental plasterwork that bespeaks a more Baroque past. The menu has subtle modern touches to a traditional range of dishes: tomato and cucumber soup, duck salad, cheddar and courgette quiche or fish quiche are good standards, but there are also variations, such as a chicken sautéed in coconut milk and basil. Staff are busy but friendly and the clientele on the younger side of working adults.

THE FRENCH MODERNS
16 Galerie Patrick Seguin

162

UP FROM THE STREETS
17 Rue Keller
- Le Souk, no. 1
- Gaëlle Barré, no. 17
- Le 18, no. 18

Turning off the rue de Charonne on to rue Keller you enter a street of regeneration that has resulted in some intelligent and highly creative tenants. Galleries, design shops, bars and ethnic restaurants now occupy once derelict spaces. Past the open pots of spices and queues of hopeful diners at Le Souk, one of the most atmospheric and intimate North African joints in Paris, you carry the scent to the tactile joy of Gaëlle Barré, full of fabulously soft mohair creations. Barré personally looks for the kind of goat that will produce her favoured material, which she turns into pure sweaters or quirky suits with printed trims and details. Shift dresses in wool with swirling patterns in mohair demonstrate her invention with a material some thought made only for snuggling. No. 18 is Le 18, Espace Créateurs, a shop and exhibitions space for young designers in clothing and accessories as well as furnishings and lighting. From avant-garde-looking skirts, bags and hats to moulded plastic furniture and futuristic, scented pendant lamps, Le 18 sets itself up as a haven for the young creatives of the Bastille and beyond.

CHANGEABLE CHIC
18 Anne Willi

13, rue Keller

This is a classic atelier and shop where the clothes are made by the designer on the premises. It has the look of a sumptuous treasure trove, for Anne Willi searches the earth for the most beautiful, luxurious fabrics, some of which might be piled on the floor when you stop by. After spending some time in Tel Aviv, where she opened a boutique, Anne Willi returned to Paris in 1998 and was an early entrepreneur on the rue Keller. Fabric in hand, she creates elegant, tunic-style long frocks, trousers, dresses and pieces that can work as two different functions. Worsted wool, felt, crepe, flannel and synthetics in deep solid colours or tulle, woven with light, gauzy details are just some of the fabrics she uses to create her elegant pieces, some of which are reversible with contrasting colours.

OF SAINTS AND SEX

19 Le Lèche Vin
13, rue Daval

Near the boulevard Richard Lenoir, the Lèche Vin appears as a kitsch bonanza with Virgin Mary standing near-lifesize in the front window and dozens of tributes – from picture-postcard-sized reproductions to figurines all aglow with fairy lights – enshrined throughout. There is also a large clown suspended from the ceiling beneath a gauzy canopy and an assortment of garden gnomes and pudgy Buddhas. This might be some reference to Pierre et Giles, but somehow the Virgin maintains her hold on the place, despite the encroaching tackiness of rue Lapin. This is a bar that saw the beginnings of the Bastille's recent hip revolution and is still one of the most charismatic, though the pornographic images in the back, given what you see in the front, might not amuse everyone.

PSYCHEDELIC

20 Le Wax

156

A DRINK AND A CHAT

21 Café de l'Industrie
16, rue St-Sabin

Among the confluence of cool urban bars and cafés around the Bastille, this is one of the better in terms of décor and one of the friendliest (though maybe not the most efficient) in terms of service. It's casual, with lots of potted plants, usually crowded but with a cheerful atmosphere, as it's not part of the usual tourist procession of drinking spots. Light meals are served but most just come for a drink and a chat or to linger in the warm red booths.

YOUTHFUL EXOTICS

22 Noir Ebène
9 and 22, rue Oberkampf

Isabelle Coeffic first started showing her creations in Paris at the age of 22 under the label Noir Ebène, referring to her own African and Indian origins. She quickly began accruing prizes and, less than a decade on, her multi-ethnic pieces are sold in concessions internationally. But her base remains here on the rue Oberkampf, opened in 2000, where her 'love of colour, shape and texture' can be seen at its fullest expression. She cites 'a mix of Indian and Japanese influences' but those are worked much more elegantly than the usual pastiche. There are flowing lines and deep rich colours, as in a

crimson kimono-style wrap and delicate patterns suggestive of Japanese watercolours. There is an abundant use of fabric with an overall flavour that is warm and exotic and reflected in the enveloping ambience of her boutique.

WINE AND ZINC
23 Le Vin de Zinc
25, rue Oberkampf

Le Vin de Zinc is everything you can ask of a clever wine bar: the space is, for once, not cramped, the food is substantial (the steak from Salers, in Auvergne, served with large French fries, shouldn't be missed) and the conversation flows as freely as the wine – which is what you'll come here for. A large blackboard lists all the famous names any wine lover knows by heart: red wines from the Domaine Gramenon (try La Sagesse or La Mémée, for instance), Beaujolais from Foillard or Métras, the fantastic Château Yvonne (a white Saumur from the Loire valley) and many more, mostly unsulphured – which means you get the pleasure without the headache.

GOLDEN AGE
24 La Flèche d'Or
102 bis, rue de Bagnolet

When Paris was circled by railways, this was a station and it retains some of its railway memorabilia and logos, and outdoor tables overlook the abandoned railway line, which is a lot more pleasant than it sounds. Transformed by students from the Beaux Arts in 1995, the interior is now a whimsical mélange of moderne and Baroque. In addition to its brunch and cocktails, La Flèche d'Or is also famous for its live music gigs featuring everything from salsa, folk and reggae to varying levels of rock. It attracts a largely young crowd at night, but lots of others flock to its outside tables and bar in the afternoon and evening, making it a lively, if decidedly crowded mix.

NEIGHBOURHOOD STAR
25 Le Villaret
142

26 Astier

44, rue Jean-Pierre-Timbaud

Here's one of Paris's most amazing wine lists – for a bistro, that is: from the cheapest to the most expensive, from around the corner (French vineyards are mainly represented, Corsica, Loire valley, very interesting prices on some Bordeaux vintages) to the New World. Add a timeless interior, elbow-to-elbow seating and a cheerful crowd, and you'll understand why the place is always fully booked. The cooking doesn't always live up to the same standard, but because the prices are perfectly fair you're unlikely to complain about your your *hachis Parmentier*, your salmon *mille-feuille* or your *crème brûlée*.

PARKSIDE SEAT

27 Bistrot Rital

1, rue des Envierges

Some say this is the most beautiful terrasse in Paris. It's certainly one of the more romantic settings, on the edge of the Parc de Belleville. The green booths and seats have a streamlined retro feeling while the old movie posters signal an association with the nearby film school. Plates of traditional Italian food and antipasti are tasty and plentiful, and the atmosphere as a whole is, well, delightful.

ARGENTINEAN JIVE

28 Le Baratin

153

29   Le Zéphyr
1, rue du Jourdain

With luck you'll be in Paris in early summer, when the city seems to breathe differently. It's an ideal time to sit at a table outside, in this fairly quiet street, under the chestnut trees, where the atmosphere is reminiscent of the countryside. But if you can't get a table on the terrace, don't worry: the inside of the Zéphyr is worth a glance or two! An authentic 1930s décor, with geometric wood designs, Naugahide benches, mosaic tiling, huge mirrors. The architectural splendour might very well distract you from the conventional food.

30   La Mère Lachaise
78, boulevard de Ménilmontant

La Mère Lachaise is not one of the latest generation of trendy, high-design bars but it offers a variety of charms. First and most attractive is the fabulous terrace on the boulevard de Ménilmontant, second is the combination of trendy, artiness of the Ménilmontant and casual ease. Inside, the two rooms are decorated in complementary, but distinctly different, themes: old and new. One room is a sort of retro hall, the other has silver upholstered walls hung with portraits by Araki. It's often crowded and boasts a fan base of celebrities and locals.

Style Traveller

sleep

Paris may still be a city of grand hotels, but recent years have seen a breath of modernity enter the realm of once chintzy and gilded establishments. If you know where to look – and what you're looking for – Paris offers a complete spectrum of guest experiences behind its noble façades – from Empire chic to lush exotica. Boutique hotels with charisma are dotted through the metropolis, and a handful of illustrious establishments have been given contemporary makeovers. The hotels below represent a select guide catering to the most refined, demanding and idiosyncratic tastes.

46 Hôtel de Vendôme

 1, place Vendôme
Rooms from €570

The façade on Paris's most exquisite *place* dates from the 17th century, but the interiors are from 1998, when the three-star hotel with 53 rooms was transformed into the current four-star accommodation with 18 luxury rooms and 11 suites, a more intimate scale than the Ritz, a few doors down. However recent the interior, Louis XIV is there in spirit. Most of the rooms and the public areas pay homage to his reign in the opulent wood and plaster decoration, crystal chandeliers, large swaths of fine fabric, paintings, gilt mirrors and antique or period-style furnishings. In other rooms Art Déco holds the stage: pale fabrics, blond woodwork and lots of mirrors. Still other rooms, like the upstairs Bar de Vendôme, have been given an English Victorian treatment. All are individually designed and no less exquisite for all their newness and their array of modern facilities. Bathrooms are expanses of coloured marble that spell out unequivocal luxury. The grand Presidential Suite penthouse on the fifth floor is a white Art Déco extravagance, complete with an outdoor terrace that overlooks the courtyard of the Sultan of Brunei – apparently he's rarely in residence. Lunch is available in the upstairs English-style bar, where formal and highly efficient barmen and waiters discharge their duties, but of course there is also 24-hour room service. Le Fumoir (p. 52), Café Marly (p. 151) and Grand Véfour (p. 136) are but a few of the fine eating establishments within a jewel's throw away.

Hotel Square

30
17 3, rue de Boulainvilliers
Rooms from €240

The original incarnation is in Monaco overlooking the sea. Here, opposite the Radio France building, the view is less dramatic from the pavement but the Seine is only a few steps away. Opened in 1997, the Hotel Square and Zebra Square restaurant were conceived by proprietor and restaurateur Patrick Derderian, who enlisted a team of designers and artists to create the art-filled interiors. From the door handles and bronze lamps by Eric Schmitt to rosewood furniture by Philippe Hurel and rugs by Christian Duc to the variations on the square motif by Pierre Bonnefille, whose work also appears in the Café Marly (see p. 151), the hotel reflects Derderian's personal preoccupation with original art. The 18-metre-high skylit stair hall and first-floor gallery are devoted to the display of artworks.

With its grey granite and strips of mirrored windows, the façade appears more corporate than the interiors, which, though minimal, are enlivened by many geometric touches and splashes of colour, like the bold red sofa in the entrance hall and the red accents in the first-floor salon, which is next to the gallery space and makes a good place to relax before an evening out.

The rooms (22, including two deluxe rooms and four suites) feature more of Philippe Hurel's elegant rosewood furniture and other individual touches, as well as lots of horizontal- and vertical-striped fabrics, which Derderian chose for their 'warm geometries'. Bathrooms are covered in Carrara marble and mirror, more straight geometry. The downstairs bar with more pieces by Bonnefille and Schmitt is a mixture of British – leather Chesterfields, high-backed period-style chairs – and dance club – dark blue supersuede upholstered walls and a DJ station that gets going later in the evenings. For a different artistic experience, visit the nearby Parc André Citroën (p. 36) and the Fondation Le Corbusier (p. 38).

SECRET GARDEN

14 | **Hôtel des Grandes Ecoles**
6 | 75, rue du Cardinal-Lemoine
Rooms from €120

Hidden behind a green door from the bustle of the Latin Quarter, and with a walkway leading in from the street into a courtyard surrounded by lovingly tended flower beds overflowing with colour, this classic hotel, a collection of pretty white and pink buildings sits in a secluded and unexpected country-cottage setting. There are tables outside where guests can have tea or breakfast in good weather, and the 51 rooms on four levels are arranged around the garden and small drive, so many overlook both, although there isn't much wheeled traffic to worry about here. The ladies at the reception desk are extremely pleasant and accommodating and are well used to speaking English and other languages. Rooms are all decorated in white and pastel floral or document-patterned textiles, perhaps a little ornate for some tastes but indubitably beautifully arranged and cared for – and perfectly in keeping with the urban-garden motif. The breakfast room, with its piano, lace tablecloths and cut flowers, is as pleasant as any tea-room.

One of the many good points of the location is its position away from the fray, and the picturesque Place de la Contrescarpe is just steps away, as is the café-rich rue Mouffetard, one of Paris' oldest streets, beloved by Hemingway. It's lost some of its old charm but is still a nice place for a casual stroll. This isn't a glamorous or very fashionable address, nor is it trying to be, but its pleasant seclusion, overall charm, inexpensive prices and the friendly attitude of its staff will guarantee the popularity of this oasis of country charm for a long time to come.

78 **Hôtel du Bourg Tibourg**

18 19, rue du Bourg-Tibourg
Rooms from €200

A crushed-velvet-lined lift, striped silk-lined walls, a forest of textures and colours wrapped, draped, gathered and set off with silky fringes – so much dramatic embellishment packed into such a small scale, but that is very much part of the cosy charm of the Bourg Tibourg. Paris's pre-eminent design family, the Costes, have pulled out all the stops in their new, 31-room hotel, formerly the Rivoli Notre Dame, in the heart of the Marais. Famed designer Jacques Garcia has combined Gothic, Oriental, French Empire and a bit of Victorian to ensure that this is an intimate hotel experience that will leave a lasting visual and sensuous impression. Every room is a unique pleasure, with beds draped in dark-coloured taffeta or silk complete with giant tassels. Low lighting and deep hues give the rooms the feeling of a richly appointed medieval garret or the tent of a desert prince. The castle theme is even more apparent in the cellar breakfast room with its stone walls covered with old tapestries and red velvet curtains. Here, in some of the most atmospheric surroundings Paris has to offer, you can also enjoy a candlelit drink, play a game of chess or retreat up the winding blue-walled staircase to the plush comforts of your room, which is rather anachronistically equipped with an Internet connection. A small interior garden, designed by Camille Muller, extends the richness out of doors.

None of the extravagance will surprise those who have had the chance to visit another collaboration between the Costes and Garcia, the Hôtel Costes (p. 159), but it is the difference in scale that makes the rue du Bourg-Tibourg's embrace all the more alluring. Although there's no restaurant, you are in the heart of the Marais, packed with restaurants, bars, ambience. Places lining the rue Bourg-Tibourg, a destination in its own right, are the jewelry designs by Philip Cardon (no. 21), the cache of imported teas at Mariage Frères (no. 30) or a glass of wine across the street at the Coude Fou (no. 12).

30 **Pershing Hall**

27 49, rue Pierre-Charron
Rooms from €400

'It is the "details" in this business that make the whole beautiful', says Andrée Putman, the French designer known for her refined interiors in Paris and abroad. A Second Empire mansion in the opulent 8th arrondissement that was once the home of the American Legion is the lucky venue for, surprisingly, Putman's first hotel in the city. Named for the American General John Joseph Pershing, who stayed there during the First World War, the building has been divided into 26 supremely appointed rooms with Putman's inimitable touch evident in everything from the mauve, coffee and caramel-coloured suede chairs to the oversized bathroom sinks and muslin toiletry bags and wicker baskets. Guests are whisked away from the many distractions of the nearby Champs-Élysées through a dramatic entrance 'tunnel', with lighting that changes colour every eight minutes, to the curved, upholstered sofas and curtains of sparkling strung beads in the lobby. Contrasting with the subtlety of the furnished spaces is a lush courtyard garden with a 34-metre-high wall hung with cascades of greenery that twinkle magically at night with hundreds of tiny lights.

The rooms are dominated by beds designed to be high off the ground and seem even more so with buoyant white bedding. Gauze curtains with subtle patterns filter natural light. The palette in the bedrooms extends to subtle mauves and purples, with luxurious textures. The sense of luxury is heightened in the bathrooms, where extra-deep tubs on marble feet stand like sculpture. 'Transforming new things in the most unexpected ways' is Putman's credo, and here she is true to her word. The restaurant and lounge ooze more Putman style, which, like her other creations around the world, manage to make the minimal sumptuous by means of clean lines and rich colour and texture.

The spare restaurant and lounge décor become a backdrop for photography exhibits as well as DJ-led dancing on selected nights. The chef, Erwan Louaisal, serves traditional French cuisine nightly.

L'Hôtel

13, rue des Beaux-Arts
Rooms from €270

Dramatic, luxurious, historic and with a fabulous location in the heart of St-Germain-des-Prés, L'Hôtel is a complete experience in the way that a small luxury hotel should be. Its Directoire period elements have been meticulously restored down to the last plaster detail in the neo-classically inspired cupola, which rises up to a spectacular skylit height, with galleried walkways overlooking the hall from all six floors. The themed bedrooms have plush combinations of the fabrics and furniture for which designer Jacques Garcia (see also p. 122) has become famous, and he has lavished the same treatment on the public rooms. The restaurant is full of swags and mirrors, period pendant lamps, a fountain and thickly upholstered seating in bohemian red patterns and crisp striped taffeta. Oscar Wilde, who died in the hotel in 1900, has a room dedicated to his luxurious tastes with some touches of his Irish provenance and letters from him scattered throughout (as well as letters to him asking for payment of debts). If the hotel was anything as wonderful then as it is today, his famous last words, 'I shall have to die above my means', are easily understood. The room labelled 'Mistinguett' is an essay in Art Déco, with plenty of boldly coloured velvet and streamlined decorative objects honouring the singer's heyday in Paris. Other rooms – the Marco Polo, the St Petersburg, the Pompéienne, the Reine Hortense – are decorated in similarly extravagant fashion. The Cardinal is particularly provocative in varying shades of purple.

A hotel since 1825, the recent incarnation is only a couple of years old and gives the place real star quality. The once-abandoned underground cellar has been reclaimed and now houses a tiled sauna and intimate swimming pool lit by candelabra on the walls and, if you like, surrounded by tea lights. Two bars have been decked out in Garcia's Belle Époque fantasy dressing, like the restaurant, le Bélier, where the cuisine is well-prepared with a small and well-considered wine list.

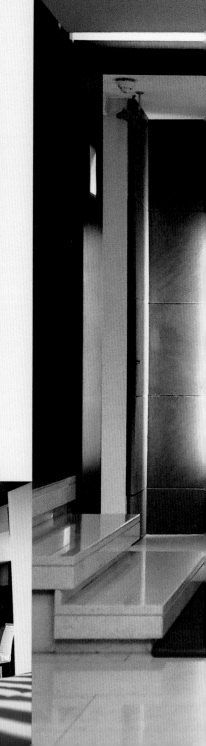

60	**Pavillon de Paris**
4	7, rue de Parme
	Rooms from €260

It is difficult to find good hotels in or adjacent to Paris's northern quarters, but that has changed with the arrival of the modern and compact Pavillon de Paris. Situated within striking distance of the Gare St-Lazare and almost on the border of the top-notch shopping district of the 8th arrondissement, the Pavillon de Paris is a townhouse hotel whose contemporary atmosphere is perhaps more suited to business travellers than romantics, but one that achieves artful elegance in its interiors and its service. The tone is set by a simple stone cube that serves as the front desk, signalling the hotel's minimalist leanings, though the rest of the place is rather less spartan, softened by dark wood and richly upholstered soft furnishings. Thirty bedrooms are decorated in the same handsome modern style, with chunks of wood and large earthy stripes. There are no suites in this egalitarian establishment, only single and double rooms, all equipped with the accessories for working or networking necessary to the business traveller, as well as some small luxuries such as candles, snacks, robes and slippers.

The ground-floor bar with its frosted glass panel and sleek décor is fine without being fussy, a place you could confidently invite a friend or colleague for a drink without feeling ostentatious. Adjoining the bar, the conservatory-style breakfast room is similarly well dressed and topped by a skylight that cheerfully illuminates the morning. There is no restaurant facility but the hotel staff will gladly arrange deliveries from local restaurants.

Whether you wish to meander around Montmartre's boutiques or bars – located a few minutes' walk away – or stroll the wide avenues of the Grands Boulevards, the Pavillon de Paris is a welcome bolthole in a largely neglected area of Paris.

30 Hôtel Duc de Saint-Simon

13 14, rue de St-Simon
Rooms from €230

The furnishings and antiques stores of the 6th and 7th arrondissements are brilliantly capped here. Through a stone archway, a quiet little patio garden leads into a treasure chest of Regency decoration inside the discreet Hôtel Duc de Saint-Simon. The Swede Göran Lindqvist bought the hotel in 1978 and set about researching its origins and associations with the famous 18th-century duke, whose meticulous diary left the fullest known account of life during the reign of Louis XIV. Today the hotel's history and charm attract a range of enthusiasts, from visiting antiques dealers to the fashionable jet-set.

Lindqvist's passion for detail becomes obvious as soon as you step into the hall, completely lined with faux *marbre*, then the lounge, where the hotel's own particular pattern of historical fabric covers walls and hangs in great sweeps alongside green velvet and red satin upholstered seating, antique furnishings and fresh flowers. Elsewhere old portraits and trompe l'oeil wall paintings complete the period feel. A treat awaits downstairs in the cellar bar and lounge, which have been converted from old wine and coal cellars and given the same whole-hearted decorative treatment, resulting in something between an antique boudoir and a louche lounge; a red-velvet corner sofa suggests long nights and long cigarette holders.

There are 29 rooms and five suites, each decorated and furnished individually but in the same period style. Some rooms have a garden view and four have private terraces, where you can have breakfast in the quiet of a private garden – the height of luxury in this much sought-after quarter. If the hotel's history interests you, and you'd like to extend your stay, mentally at least, a copy of the book (text in French and English) produced by Lindqvist with the help of the president of the Saint Simon Society is available for purchase.

eat

Thanks to falling prices and a new generation of chefs, Paris has recently, and rather swiftly, become a less expensive, less intimidating, more informal, and more open culinary destination. Many young chefs promote what food writers call 'bistronomic' venues, which feature great food in a laid-back atmosphere. For those wishing to experience (and have remembered to book before travelling) the apotheosis of gastronomy, Paris remains unrivalled: Alain Ducasse at the Plaza-Athénée, Guy Martin at the Grand Véfour and Pierre Gagnaire offer once-in-a-lifetime pleasures. Don't forget the family-run bistros, the essence of everyday cooking, which continue to thrive and reinvent themselves.

Guy Savoy

18, rue Troyon

A lover of the arts and fashion, Guy Savoy likes to say that his restaurant, recently redecorated by Jean-Michel Wilmotte (with dark African wood, beige leather and modern paintings), is nothing but a 21st-century inn — in so saying he has described in a nutshell the warmth and casualness he promotes in his exceptional establishment. And it is noteworthy that the excellent staff offer something different (with cheery greetings of 'Good evening, monsieur, good evening, madame' and other attentive details such as the placing of a napkin on your knees) and that the atmosphere is much more relaxed than in other such places. The food manages to be something between true luxury and false simplicity, with the artichoke and black truffle velouté as bridgehead. Quite often amazing, especially with the help of sommelier Eric Mancio, one of Paris's most renowned professionals.

THE CRITICS' BISTRO

46 **Chez Georges**

25 1, rue du Mail

Asked to name their favourite bistro, many of Paris's sharpest food writers choose Georges (not be be confused with the restaurant on top of the Centre Pompidou, p. 81). When you stand before the tiny wooden façade, you may wonder why, for the place looks like many others. But walk in, sit down and you'll understand what a perfect traditional bistro should look like. First, it has to do with the atmosphere, which is so French and old-fashioned you might think you've travelled back to the 1960s: an elegant though unpretentious dining room with one long, white-tableclothed stretch of tables between the mirrored walls. For food, you'll enjoy perfect herrings, foie gras, *andouillettes, petit salé*, steaks and perhaps the best French fries (!) in the city. The wine list veers towards the expensive, though that in no way diminishes Georges's timeless appeal.

TIMELESS PLEASURE
46 **Le Grand Véfour**
13 17, rue de Beaujolais

Would Victor Hugo still recognize 'his' restaurant? Certainly, though in his time it was still called 'Le Café de Chartres'. Originally built in 1784, what was to become Le Grand Véfour has welcomed absolutely everybody, from Napoléon to Colette and Jean Cocteau – most seats bear a small brass plaque commemorating some famous patron. In those days, it was probably the most beautiful restaurant in Paris and today it probably still is, mostly because it is charged with so much history and so exquisitely adorned. Against the opulent surroundings, chef Guy Martin's food has a contemporary feel, blending sophistication and rusticity. He hails from the mountains of Savoie, so you'll find earthy dishes among all the foie gras and truffle-stuffed ravioli or the famous artichoke pie (a dessert).

NEW HEIGHTS OF CUISINE
30 **Jules Verne**
26 Eiffel Tower, Champ-de-Mars

The crucial question is: will you get a table at the Eiffel Tower's second-storey restaurant? For this is a place famous for its three-month waiting list for dinner. If you've got a head for heights, a hunger for one of Paris's most breathtaking settings and if haven't made advance reservations, it's a bit less overcrowded at lunchtime. Day or night, Jules Verne is unique, with its private lift, sublime panorama over the Seine and the Trocadéro and black and grey Slavik décor, a surprisingly effective means of establishing atmosphere inside when there is so much to see outside. And let's not forget Alain Reix's cuisine, a subtle combination of terrestrial and marine flavours, quite often luxurious, as well as the perfect service and an amazing wine list whose prices reflect an affluent international clientele. Despite the throngs of tourists scaling up and down Gustave Eiffel's achievement, you will be a world away.

LOCAL ASSETS
46 **Gallopin**
26 40, rue Notre-Dame-des-Victoires

Next to the old stock exchange, the Gallopin has long been a headquarters for the brokers and journalists who work near by. But it is mainly one of the city's most beautiful brasseries, with an ageless 1880s décor (superb mahogany panelling, mirrors, glass roof, brass lamps and a bar for those who just want to read a newspaper), originally created by Gustave Gallopin for his establishment in London (his wife was English), the Stock Exchange Luncheon Bar, which still adorns its Paris reincarnation. Regulars say that it is impossible to find a more Parisian place than this. Food is as traditional as you can imagine, which means that you can enjoy dipping into a huge seafood platter before indulging in some hot *crêpes Suzette,* naturally sprinkled with Grand Marnier and set alight in front of you. Magic, eternal, unique.

ÉLÉGANCE SUPRÊME
78 L'Ambroisie
10 9, place des Vosges

If you are fond of food, you will most probably have heard of chefs like Alain Ducasse or Bernard Loiseau, from Burgundy. But does the name of Bernard Pacaud ring a bell? If not, you don't know what you've been missing. This very discreet man runs one of Paris's best restaurants – some would even say *the* best restaurant – set in one of Paris's best locations. The moment you arrive under the magnificent arcades of the 17th-century place des Vosges and step into the hushed elegance of the Viennese-inflected interior designed by François-Joseph Graf, you will begin to sense what makes this place so special. L'Ambroisie is simply the epitome of classic French cuisine, but with a twist of modernity. Sharp flavours, high prices, a truly memorable experience. Reservations should be made at least one month in advance.

GLOBAL FUSION COMES TO PARIS
30 Spoon, Food & Wine
28 12, rue de Marignan

When Alain Ducasse opened his bistro at the end of 1998, many looked on it as though it had landed from another planet. The star chef's (see also p. 145) astute idea was to introduce a do-it-yourself fusion-food menu where one could mix and match dishes to one's heart's desire: in Paris, perhaps in the world, this was brand new, something that had never been done before. Hence, the place became immediately popular among a fashionable jet-set crowd, drawn by the playful Asian-, French-, Italian- and American-inspired menu. From Thai soup to pasta with a superb tomato marmalade, from the pan-seared squid with satay sauce and wok-sautéed vegetables to a bubble gum ice-cream: a lot to discover, a lot to savour and a lot to learn from a French chef's take on global fusion. There's also a lot to drink, with a wine list that boasts an unprecedentedly high percentage of New World wines. Reservations should be made one month in advance.

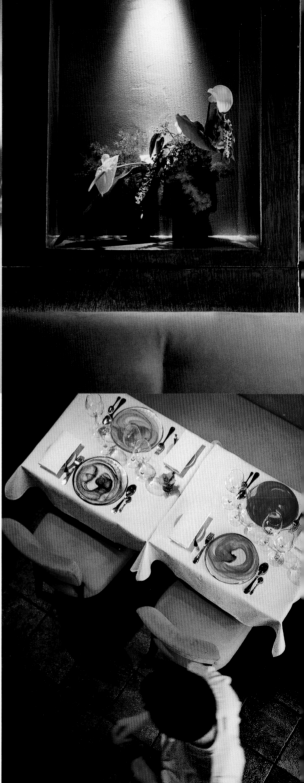

30 L'Astrance

14 4, rue Beethoven

It was something like love at first sight. When chef Pascal Barbot and maître d' Christophe Rohat (both formerly at Alain Passard's restaurant, L'Arpège) opened their tiny (fewer than a dozen tables), elegant restaurant in 2001, every single Parisian food lover begged for a table. L'Astrance, named after a flower from Auvergne, instantly became the city's best newcomer for years, with its modern, creative and sharp cooking (the avocado and crab ravioli is one of their most famous dishes). Make sure to let them handle your meal and you'll most certainly have a great time. Adopt the same attitude with wines: Monsieur Rohat knows best. Reservations should be made at least one month in advance.

46 **Lucas-Carton**

7 9, place de la Madeleine

There is probably no chef in France as passionately involved in matching wine and food as philosopher-chef Alain Senderens, who took over from the eponymous Carton family some years ago. Each dish here is served with the glass of wine considered the most suitable. Did you perhaps choose the Iranian caviar with white onions cooked in clay and Italian pistachios? Your maître d' will strongly suggest a 1993 Dom Pérignon. The wild duck with caramelized leeks, mango and ginger? Why not consider a glass of a 1995 Clos Vougeot? These alchemies are presented in one of Paris's most breathtaking décors (listed as a historic monument), an authentic and flamboyant 1905 Art Nouveau masterpiece — hand-sculpted Jugendstil wood panelling by Planel, sinuous bronze wall-lamps and other ornamental marvels for your satisfied senses to enjoy.

Dining beneath the chestnut trees, on the large terrace of the Napoléon III pavilion overlooking manicured lawns and flowerbeds, is pure bliss. Set in the heart of the Bois de Boulogne in the western end of the city, Le Pré Catalan is one of the most romantic spots you could find – a culinary journey into nature not far from the city centre. Chef Frédéric Anton, who has worked several years with Joël Robuchon, has brought something essential to this restaurant with his new classic cuisine: try the small jellied velvet swimming crabs, the tender and almost melting baby carrots with ginger sauce or the John Dory glazed with maple syrup, and you'll understand this man is simply a master. Great wine list with some clever selections, and near-perfect service.

98 Le Villaret

25 13, rue Ternaux

What used to be a fabulous neighbourhood bistro with clever cooking is becoming, year after year, a truly ambitious restaurant (in the positive sense of the word). But new visitors needn't worry, the overall style hasn't changed at all: Le Villaret still has a laid-back atmosphere and a funky clientele, with its strange mix of hip young Asians, grannies from next door, wine lovers ordering five bottles at a time (the wine list is constantly improving) and men in white collars with loosened ties. Though prices have risen in recent years, the place still draws numerous patrons (reservations essential) who know that quality and taste will be part of the deal. Self-taught chef Olivier Gaslain likes tweaking classic French cooking, though there's little likelihood you will bump into a Camembert pizza or other such fusion silliness here. It also benefits from being open until very late at night.

30 Pierre Gagnaire

39 Hôtel Balzac, 6, rue Balzac

Don't say 'I do not remember ordering this' when the staff bring six or seven small dishes to your table. That's just the beginning of every meal at Pierre Gagnaire's: wildly creative tapas are offered as a kind of welcome present, to give you a first glimpse of his kind of cooking. Poetic, sincere, intuitive and spontaneous, he is also capable of surprising even those who are frequent visitors to this modern grey-painted and wooden-clad dining room. One can never tell what a meal will be like here, as Pierre Gagnaire sometimes changes his menus or his recipes on the same day as he presents them. All you need to know is that his cooking often blends unexpected flavours, textures and products, and that it swings like bebop. Just let the staff handle your journey; it could very well be an unforgettable one.

| 30 | **Petrossian** |
| 29 | 18, boulevard de La Tour-Maubourg |

The man who put Petrossian on every food-lover's itinerary and one of Paris's most wildly creative pâtissiers is Philippe Conticini. One sample of the dessert he calls 'Teasers, five explosions of taste' and you'll realize you never had such a sweet experience, a devastating medley of soft and crispy textures, coulis, emulsions, spices and very possibly more. You might also appreciate some savoury pleasures, including his risotto with caramel and foie gras or the smoked salmon with a white salmon sherbet ... If that's not enough, caviar, which has been sold in the downstairs premises since 1920s, makes an appearance on the menu. Now largely run by Conticini's sous-chef, Petrossian is thoroughly unusual and most exciting.

| 14 | **La Régalade** |
| 33 | 49, avenue Jean-Moulin |

Ten years ago a young chef from the southwest of France, Yves Camdeborde, who previously worked with some of the biggest names of Paris's grand hotels, decided to change paths. He opened his own place, a small and noisy bistro far from everything and started offering a limited-choice, fixed-price menu: he was one of the first to do so and success was immediate. Today, his old-fashioned provincial bistro is still regularly taken by storm at lunch and dinner (they sometimes do three dinner sittings to satisfy the hungry crowd). Reservations are essential if you want to taste one of Paris's most exciting seasonal cuisines, apparently simple but very often luxurious : superb game, foie gras in breadcrumbs, cassoulet, black *boudin* from Béarn, supplemented by a short and clever wine list – and a huge helping of atmosphere.

L'Arpège
84, rue de Varenne

Even Alain Passard's biggest fans will tell you his restaurant is one of the most expensive in Paris: the exciting but for many almost unattainable *menu dégustation* is to blame, as well as the ambitious wine list. But if money is no object, and you find yourself hungry after a stroll around the Musée Rodin (p. 33), l'Arpège is definitely a must-go, particularly if you have vegetarian inclinations. Passard decided a couple of years ago to focus on vegetables, which he grows in his own personal vegetable garden in Anjou (but he also serves seafood and poultry). Try the sweet onions with parmesan and black pepper, little beets with a syrupy balsamic vinegar and black truffles or a carrot and verbena consommé; you'll feel as if you never tasted vegetables before. A captivating, bold and unique gastronomic experience – and worth every Euro.

Ze Kitchen Galerie
4, rue des Grands-Augustins

Those people who have travelled the world might feel they've seen something quite similar in other global capitals … 15 years ago. But a place like Ze Kitchen Galerie in Paris is something new: it has a modernist, white-washed loft-like décor, paintings on the walls and an open kitchen you can freely peer into through a glass panel (a genuine novelty in the city). Located in the 6th arrondissement's high concentration of antiques and furniture galleries, it has a relaxed and peaceful atmosphere. Food, created by chef William Ledeuil, complements this mood with a vocabulary of his own: playful, sharp, quick-paced and open-minded (plenty of Asian herbs and spices), with a destructured 'carte', allowing one to choose pasta and soup instead of the traditional starter followed by main course followed by dessert. Marinated raw fish, meats or vegetables '*à la planche*', creative desserts: an artful place, an artful location, an artful chef – worth many visits.

'French excellence': Alain Ducasse's buzzword is ultimately quite simple. And how does France's star chef manage to maintain such a standard? He simply chooses the best money can buy (from salt to butter, lobster to lamb, poultry to asparagus, and one of the few restaurants in Paris where you can taste the horrendously expensive Italian white truffle in the winter), has hired the best staff one can imagine (from chef to sommeliers, maître d' to waiters) and has asked young designer Patrick Jouin to create what is currently one of the most surprising décors of such upper-class venues (Louis XV–style chairs, painted metal-grey, combined with modern touches such as the holographic lighting effects produced by a huge organza veil). Such perfection is hard to find.

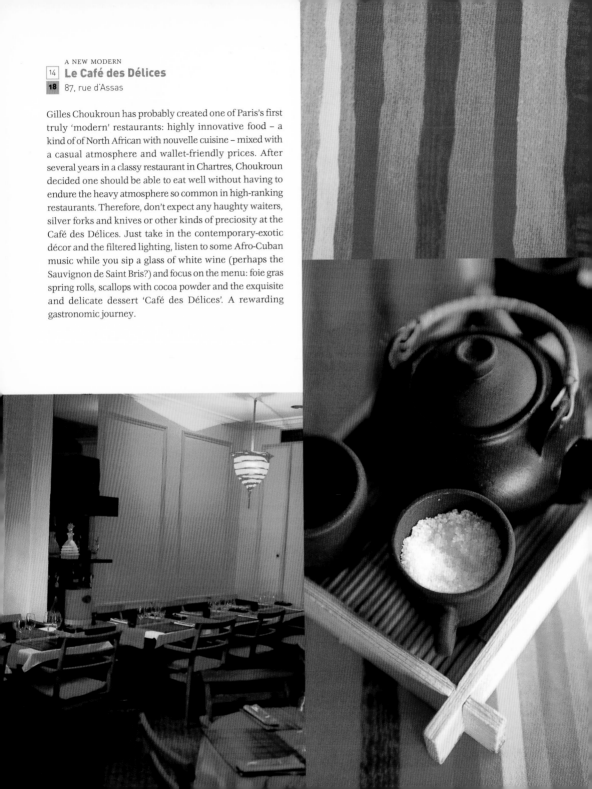

14 **Le Café des Délices**

18 87, rue d'Assas

Gilles Choukroun has probably created one of Paris's first truly 'modern' restaurants: highly innovative food – a kind of of North African with nouvelle cuisine – mixed with a casual atmosphere and wallet-friendly prices. After several years in a classy restaurant in Chartres, Choukroun decided one should be able to eat well without having to endure the heavy atmosphere so common in high-ranking restaurants. Therefore, don't expect any haughty waiters, silver forks and knives or other kinds of preciosity at the Café des Délices. Just take in the contemporary-exotic décor and the filtered lighting, listen to some Afro-Cuban music while you sip a glass of white wine (perhaps the Sauvignon de Saint Bris?) and focus on the menu: foie gras spring rolls, scallops with cocoa powder and the exquisite and delicate dessert 'Café des Délices'. A rewarding gastronomic journey.

RENEWED CLASSIC

30 35 Lasserre

17, avenue Franklin-Roosevelt

For many years, dining at Lasserre was like visiting granny: stuffy atmosphere and staff, old-fashioned food — one of Paris's most historic restaurants had grown boring, despite the presence over the years of such regular customers as Salvador Dalí and André Malraux. But all this was well before the arrival of chef Jean-Louis Nomicos, one of Alain Ducasse's disciples. If you enjoy Belle Époque restaurants with a host of monumental flower arrangements and a 'grand-bourgeois' ambience, be assured, the décor is intact. Nomicos has brought a personal touch into the kitchen, along with southern Mediterranean flavours, very often brilliant. And while you're tasting his cuisine, you will experience Lasserre's very special ritual: the opening by the staff of the retractable ceiling for enjoying the stars and sky above. Jacket and tie required.

drink

Going out for a drink in Paris is an experience you'll find hard to match in almost any other city in the world. In the land of the flâneur, it is about using your eyes and ears as much as your palate, for the best drinking spots are steeped in the French sensitivity to beauty, style and ambience. Romantic images of Parisian café society, as clichéd as they have become, are not entirely untrue. From grand, Belle Époque hotel bars to the latest designer restaurant space; from funky revival cafés to revered neighbourhood establishments; from cocktails and wine to coffee and tea, the places where Parisians (and lucky foreigners) go to sit and sip and look and listen cover a range of moods and moments – always with panache.

14 **La Mosquée de Paris**

4 39, rue Geoffroy-St-Hilaire

If you're planning a visit to the spectacular Jardin des Plantes, then it's also a good time to take in the 1920s mosque built in Hispano-Moorish style by three French architects and decorated by numerous North African artisans. Featuring lacey Moorish patterns in intricately carved wood screens, decorative tilework and lighting and ornate cupolas, the mosque also has beautifully kept patio gardens. You might enjoy the *hammam* or have traditional mint tea at the café/tea-room in a plant-filled courtyard, itself reminiscent of a Mughal palace.

TEA CEREMONIES

14 **La Maison des Trois Thés**

5 33, rue Gracieuse

Tea is becoming more popular in Paris, though, as you might expect, in a refined and sometimes even *haute* manner. While smart hotels like the Hôtel de Crillon offer posh afternoon tea with cakes in the Winter Garden, something different is on offer at La Maison des Trois Thés, where Taiwanese proprietress Yu Hui Tseng, a tea-master, is on a mission to promote the ancient *gong fu* ceremony in Europe, along with a genuine appreciation of tea. Hundreds of varieties, from the humble jasmine to the rare (and dear) oolong are available in her tea-room.

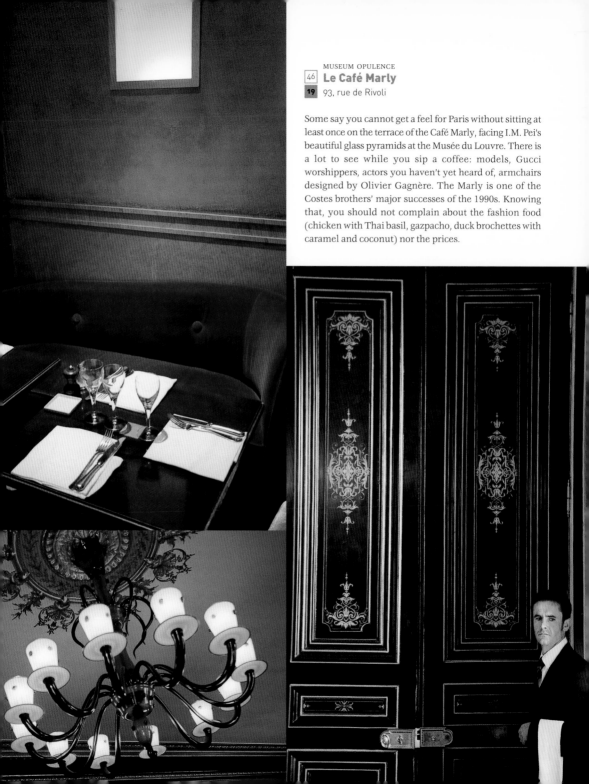

46 Le Café Marly

19 93, rue de Rivoli

Some say you cannot get a feel for Paris without sitting at least once on the terrace of the Café Marly, facing I.M. Pei's beautiful glass pyramids at the Musée du Louvre. There is a lot to see while you sip a coffee: models, Gucci worshippers, actors you haven't yet heard of, armchairs designed by Olivier Gagnère. The Marly is one of the Costes brothers' major successes of the 1990s. Knowing that, you should not complain about the fashion food (chicken with Thai basil, gazpacho, duck brochettes with caramel and coconut) nor the prices.

FUGITIVE OENOPHILIA

78 **Le Verre Volé**

35 67, rue de Lancry

Wine bar, wine shop and microbistro rolled into one. This is what makes 'the stolen glass' such an unusual place. Since the word has begun to spread out of the Canal St Martin area and across Paris, you'll need to book one of the four or five tables if you want to eat or be seated to enjoy some of the finest wines of the moment (the white Coteaux d'Aix from Château Bas, the Vinsobres from the Domaine Gramenon in the Rhône valley) with a simple plate of cheese or some oysters. The tiny locale doesn't inhibit enjoyment, however – it can be wild from time to time.

CLASSIC WINE SHOP

46 **Legrand Filles et Fils**

9 1, rue de la Banque

When you enter you're bound to spend the first hour simply admiring the place. Legrand Filles et Fils is pure beauty, one of Paris's oldest *épiceries fines*, run by the same family for decades. Consider the candies, the ports, the dozens of wines, then grab a seat at the bar, which is in the brand-new area of the store. If you want to discover some great wines, just ask for one of the 15 served by the glass, from red Sancerre to Chilean Cabernet-Sauvignon. Food? Pleasing plates of goat cheese, charcuteries or foie gras, all coming from the best producers in the country.

30 **Les Coteaux**

3 26, boulevard Garibaldi

As everyone knows, the setting for this tiny 'bistro à vin', right in front of an overground subway, isn't the most glamorous. But no one cares because this is one of the city's most engaging wine joints, the kind where the buffs go for serious tasting. Ask the owner to locate the perfect bottle: he knows Beaujolais better than anyone (he even blends some vintages with the wine growers). His accompanying cooking is hearty, based mostly on traditional Lyonnaise specialities: try the *tablier de sapeur*, the charcuterie plate, *andouillette* or the fantastic cheeses.

98 **Le Baratin**

28 3, rue Jouye-Rouve

Take no notice if you hear a Spanish-accented woman's voice yelling from the kitchen: that's Raquel, the cook, from Argentina. For Le Baratin (French for 'jive') is one of Belleville's most famous wine bars, unexpected, unusual, bohemian and engaging – definitely the place to go if you want to grasp something of the eastern Parisian state of mind. Don't forget to book a table (the place is always full and smoky) to try one of the numerous wines by the glass (the wine list is purely remarkable) and one of Raquel's Franco-Argentinean dishes.

Passage de Retz

9, rue Charlot

A former toy factory in the Marais has been turned into a clean and bright contemporary art gallery that now makes a pleasant stop off the rue Charlot and hosts local artistic happenings. Entering through the large wood doors into a quiet courtyard, you head right into the small museum shop selling funky items and books. Next to the bookshop is a little 1950s-inspired café created by smooth designer Christian Biecher. Just a few blocks away from the Marais' more touristed streets, it's a bright, quiet and groovy place for coffee and snacks.

le petit café

30 **Bar at the Plaza-Athénée**

37 25, avenue Montaigne

Some, even some Parisians, describe this as the most beautiful bar in Paris. Beneath Murano glass chandeliers, high, grey Louis XV–style stools line the long, transparent bar that glows like a slab of blue ice. The décor is the work of Patrick Jouin, who redid the interior after the bar was destroyed by fire in 2000 – one reason, perhaps, for the icy feel. The wood panelling and chandeliers survived, and the stage was set for the models, actresses and rock stars who like to revel in its glory. Sip a champagne mojito and watch the limousines arrive; save the jelly shots for later.

98 **Le Wax**

20 15, rue Daval

Wax nostalgic about a bygone age in this groovy trip of a bar, a safe distance from rue Lapin. Lounging in the canary-yellow, moulded plastic benches or cool, modern, white leather and chrome swivel chairs, among plastic bubble lights that look like orange jelly and curvy purple niches, evening revellers at Le Wax will enjoy the atmosphere of a forbidden but highly tempting pleasure den. Be sure to have a look across the street at the unsigned space of purple and glass walls, featuring clothes, objects, jewelry and art by emerging French designers and artists.

30 40 La Cantine du Faubourg

105, rue du Faubourg-St-Honoré

Young, trendy, crowded, laid back, huge, colourful, restaurant, bar, lounge – what else do you need to know? This recently opened all-round night spot is worth a glance for its *mélange des genres*, which will make you wonder if you're in an art gallery, a restaurant or a night club (all of the above). From 11 am to 4 am, you should have enough time to check out the sculpted slate bar, the screen walls, the subtle light show, the hard-boiled egg or the caviar, the *pot au feu* or the chicken teriyaki, the guest table for 14 and the open kitchen.

It's the large illuminated dance floor and the music of well-known Parisian DJ Claude Challe that gets this downstairs club going. Indian-inspired décor by Jonathan Amar is chic to some, borderline kitsch to others, but there's no question about the ambience. Unlike most clubs that are open until 4 in the morning, Nirvana also includes an upmarket restaurant run by two young chefs who turn out fusion cuisine. Try *le Kama-sutra aux pétales de roses* for dessert or the less exotic late-night munchies.

Started by the same team who opened the China Club is a grand themed re venture that evokes a bygone era and p ground-floor restaurant begins in the s evolving to colonial chic upstairs in the portraits of august Europeans altern Chinese in revolutionary dress. Wid palms, white tablecloths mixed with and cigars recall the Jazz Age speake down the road from the Opéra Bastille

SECOND-EMPIRE SEDUCTION
46 | Hôtel Costes
11 | 239, rue St-Honoré

It's been described as everything from Second Empire bordello to just plain over-the-top, but the Hôtel Costes has to be seen to be believed. Interior designer Jacques Garcia (see also p. 122) displays the full range of his extravagant historic-fantasy taste in the bar and restaurant area. The miles of striped, embossed, tasselled, tented and draped fabric, the forest of columns, the lighting and atmosphere is discreet *haute* meets hallucinogenic – even if it weren't frequented by names in fashion, film and the media. It's discreet because despite the décor's exuberance the tables are all somehow intimate, tucked between columns or behind a bit of curtain or nestled beneath the courtyard umbrellas. For drinking in a bit of theatre, Hôtel Costes is a superlative experience.

shop

In a city that defines style not only in the fickle fashion world but in furniture and product design, shopping is a near-spiritual experience. Where to begin the quest? Furniture from Louis XV to Jean Michel Franck to Philippe Starck or the newest crop of hip French designers, all available from a host of enthusiastic and knowledgeable dealers? Stunningly attired boutiques that lure you in, whether they're selling *chaussures* or chocolates, perfumes or *patisserie*. The fashion empires of the Champs-Élysées and St-Germain-des-Prés are irresistible, but so are the young, independent craftspeople of the Marais and Montmartre, who produce their handcrafted goods in boutiques where one-off products can be purchased directly from the creator.

Galerie Patrick Seguin

34, rue de Charonne

Specializing in French furniture and objects from the 1950s, the gallery carries pieces by Le Corbusier, Alexandre Noll, Georges Jouve, Jean Royère, Charlotte Perriand and Serge Mouille, and there is a particular focus on Jean Prouvé. Don't be fooled by the seemingly limited arrangement in the rue de Charonne; there is a much larger showroom nearby on the rue des Taillandiers, to which you will be happily escorted for a look around. The showroom is due for a design overhaul by Jean Nouvel in 2003. Seguin also hosts regular exhibitions.

Galerie Yves Gastou

12, rue Bonaparte

A rosewood-and-glass bookcase made in 1936 by Jacques Adnet, a 1940 André Arbus commode, a pair of violet silk bergères by René Prou – just a few of the French treasures from the 1930s and 1940s at the Galerie Yves Gastou. Jean-Michel Franck, Gilbert Poillerat and Emilio Terry also figure in his collection, housed in a space designed by Ettore Sotsass. Gastou is a consummate collector whose search began in the 1970s, the point up to which the pieces run. It is the earlier periods, however, that make his impeccable showroom a necessary stop for collectors.

78 **Sentou Galerie**

12 18 and 24, rue du Pont Louis-Philippe;
29, rue François-Miron; 26, boulevard Raspail

The Sentou collection made its name under Robert Sentou, who began selling Isamu Noguchi lamps and exhibited the soon-to-be-famous staircase by Roger Tallon. Pierre Romanet, who took over from Sentou in the 1980s, has expanded the range and championed new designers such as Tsé & Tsé and Christain Biecher through stocking their pieces and holding exhibitions. He's now known as a patron of new French design, stocking the work of Frédéric Sofia, Pierre Paulin, Jérôme Gauthier, Robert le Héros and David Design.

MODERN FRENCH AND NEW-DESIGN FURNITURE

14 **Alexandre Biaggi**

26 14, rue de Seine

Alexandre Biaggi has been dealing in antique furniture since he hired a stand at the Marché aux Puces in 1987. Since 1989 he has had his own shop selling French 19th- and 20th-century furniture and objects, which he has refined even further to French design from the 1930s, 1940s and 1950s – Jean-Michel Frank, André Arbus and Jacques Adnet, as well as Paul Dupré-Lafon, Serge Roch, Jean Royère and Jacques Quinet, to name a few. In addition, he is the exclusive dealer in the work of contemporary designers Hervé van der Straeten and Nicolas Aubagnac.

The play of light in Rei Kawakubo's paean to minimalism somehow echoes the subtle, sensual distinctions of scent. Following the success of her Commes des Garçons fashion label (a similarly hard-edged, red shop at 54, rue du Faubourg-St-Honoré), Kawakubo launched five perfumes, which are all displayed here to great effect along white-enamelled steel units. The pink-coloured glass front designed by London's Future Systems changes from opaque to transparent; the colour is taken from the packaging of 'Odeur 71'.

Yann Schalburg and Marie-Christine van Dame's shop is a perfume collector's dream, filled with rare, cut-crystal pieces, from turn-of-the-century smelling salts bottles – meant to combat the fainting often brought on from tight corsetry – to boxes for creams, hairpins, soaps and ointments all made in the days before plastics, when such cosmetics came in their own specially designed vessels. Pieces by Baccarat, St Louis and Val Saint Lambert accompany perfumes by Guerlain and Houbigant. Other prizes include 1930s Lalique crystal containers.

Exclusive jewelry designer Joel Rosenthal has always had a passion for perfume, to the extent that he started collecting classic scents. He created his first fragrance, Golconda, in the late 1980s, but it was available only in its special Baccarat bottle through selected outlets. In October 2001 he launched five more fragrances in this tiny, mauve-velvet-wrapped shop, which displays the fragrances and bottles he has designed for them like jewels. Rosenthal intended that the experience would leave an impression even if clients don't buy anything.

Frédéric Malle wanted to revolutionize perfume-making, so he hired nine reputable perfume-makers and gave them carte blanche to produce original, complex scents. These mystery 'noses', formerly unknown because of their associations with large perfumeries, now have their names attached to the scents created under the auspices of Malle's Editions, which he says he produces like a publisher. Interiors were designed by Malle with his friend and 'the godmother of the shop', Andrée Putman, together with her protégé, architect Olivier de Lempereur.

30
4

PARIS'S OLDEST DEPARTMENT STORE
Au Bon Marché
24, rue de Sèvres

Department stores are rarely like this Left Bank institution. First, it's a pleasure to behold: the metalwork was designed by Gustave Eiffel and the two buildings maintain their *fin-de-siècle* and 1920s decoration. Émile Zola was inspired by its social scene. And it remains one of Paris's most fashionable places to shop. Women's and menswear sections feature the latest designs, from Gaultier to Galliano, as well as the store's less expensive own brand. Newly revamped perfume and lingerie departments are brilliantly stocked with those goods for which the French have long been famous. (Convenient phones in the lingerie dressing rooms mean you can ring an assistant to bring another size.) The food hall, or Grande Epicerie, is as grand and as beautiful as it is tempting. And there's no need to worry about carrying packages, as the store will gladly deliver to your hotel. The Square Boucicaut across the street is a good place to rest and breathe deeply after a shopping frenzy.

14 **Christian Tortu**

25 17, rue des Quatre-Vents

You've bought the book, *Sensational Bouquets*, now witness the flowers, inhale the designer fragrance, size up his line of vases. When Christian Tortu says that he's inspired by nature, he means thorns and all. His floral arrangements, used by fashion houses such as Chanel and Dior, are as likely to contain prickly brambles as roses and are as full of fruits, vegetables, wood or leaves as of buds. An 'arrangement' might be a potted topiary hedge with large cut-outs or a collection of spicy *oranges des osages*. He now also makes soaps, candles and beauty creams.

SWEET ARTS

14 **Pierre Hermé**

28 72, rue Bonaparte
Tea-room: 33, rue Marbeuf

To know him is to love his creations: melt-in-your-mouth macaroons, apple-and-almond milk tart, 'velvet heart' cake – like beautiful still lifes that you can eat. All Paris is wild about Pierre Hermé, as you can tell by the queue stretching out of his tiny jewel-box shop designed by Yann Pennor, especially on a Friday afternoon. He is uniquely creative with chocolate. He works like a fashion designer, creating 'collections' by season, and has recently opened a tea-room off the Champs-Élysées.

Isabel Marant

16, rue de Charonne

Though her clothes are now sold in selected outlets around the world, Isabel Marant set up her first shop far from the fashion-following crowds of the Left Bank. The gently rustic, wood-floored boutique on the busy rue de Charonne carries her ever-popular collection of elegant but down-to-earth women's fashions in fabrics that are flattering and pleasing to the skin. Travels to Africa and India have influenced the clever draping that is her passion, but the young designer (born 1967) also has a whimsical side and a knack for surprising combinations, which she showed in the themes of her winter 2001 collection – 'modern dance and fencing' – with white, quilted jackets and flared-silk trouser outfits. The shop is filled with items that are less challenging: pretty, scoop-necked dresses and T-shirts exhibiting a taste for flounces, 1970s-style combinations of peasant-style tapestry skirts topped with corduroy blazers, ruffled skirts and tops in heavy crepes, trouser suits in corduroy or hefty cotton velour and heavy cotton jackets, all in complementary earth shades with the occasional gathered wrist or high neck.

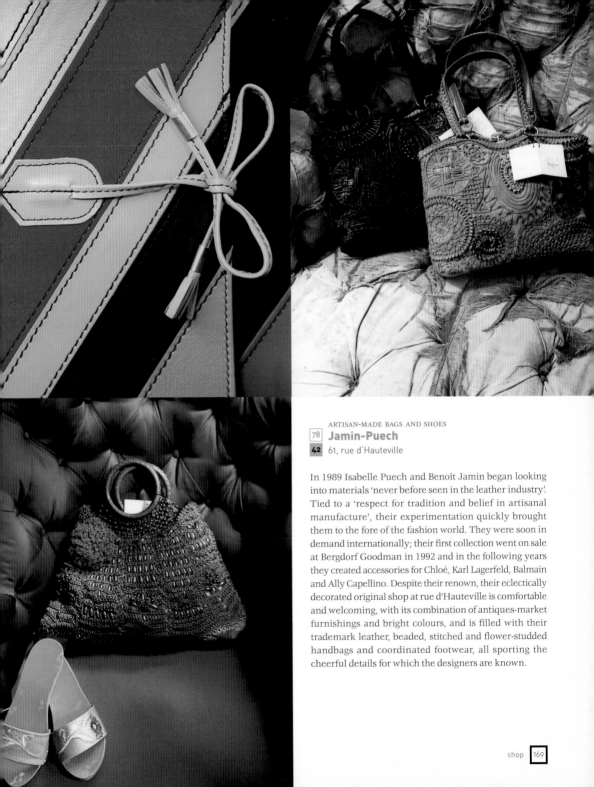

ARTISAN-MADE BAGS AND SHOES
78 **Jamin-Puech**
42 61, rue d'Hauteville

In 1989 Isabelle Puech and Benoît Jamin began looking into materials 'never before seen in the leather industry'. Tied to a 'respect for tradition and belief in artisanal manufacture', their experimentation quickly brought them to the fore of the fashion world. They were soon in demand internationally; their first collection went on sale at Bergdorf Goodman in 1992 and in the following years they created accessories for Chloé, Karl Lagerfeld, Balmain and Ally Capellino. Despite their renown, their eclectically decorated original shop at rue d'Hauteville is comfortable and welcoming, with its combination of antiques-market furnishings and bright colours, and is filled with their trademark leather, beaded, stitched and flower-studded handbags and coordinated footwear, all sporting the cheerful details for which the designers are known.

Jacques Le Corre has been working as a designer since the late 1980s but set up this streamlined, funky boutique only in October 2001; you'll know it by the large fish on the walls. After a spell working in Japan, Le Corre came back to Paris to promote his distinctive line of hats, handbags and shoes. The raffia hats in natural hues or bold solid colours are amazingly stylish, despite their humble materials and their ability to bounce back after you have folded, twisted or smashed them in a suitcase. Le Corre has a determined artisanal approach, which means bags are finely detailed in an array of designs that combine style and practicality, with a range of flattering shoes to match.

14 **Peggy Huyn Kinh**

13 11, rue Coëtlogon

As the bright orange theme suggests, this is the headquarters of a bold designer who isn't afraid to stand out. Having worked as artistic director for Madame Grès, Pierre Balmain and Céline and as a scarf and leather designer for Cartier, Peggy Huyn Kinh ventured to produce her own label in 1996 and opened this shop in 2000. A heavy oak floor and leather-upholstered walls offset her creations, in crocodile, python and wild boar skin, which are striking even from the street. Rectilinear shapes frame her vibrant colours – orange, red and blue.

SEXY STILETTOS

46 **Rodolphe Ménudier**

4 14, rue de Castiglione

Space is at a premium in this luxury shopping parade near the place Vendôme but designer Christophe Pillet has made a virtue of the intimacy with an interior that is as sleek and sexy as Rodolphe Ménudier's shoes. Having worked for Lagerfeld, Paco Rabanne, Christian Lacroix and Chanel, Ménudier certainly has the classic pedigree, but there is a a rock 'n' roll edge to his stilettos, cork heels and fringes, not to mention his knee-high and over-the-knee boots, with distinctive details, such as saucy straps, leather spaghetti laces and buckles.

Dominique Picquier Paris

78

27 10, rue Charlot

It would be hard for anyone who appreciates colour and fabric to walk by Dominique Picquier's shop and not step inside. A textile designer with a penchant for plant life, Picquier specializes in monochrome canvas with abstract floral patterns printed in or reversed out of the background. 'I would like people to see my collection as a tribute to nature in the city,' she says. Bolts of fabrics as well as throws, bedspreads, cushion covers, curtains and an array of khaki-toned bags with heavy-duty stitched handles offer a unique blend of beauty and strength.

Dominique Kieffer designs fabrics and objects to do with
fabric, such as cushions and throws, but that doesn't begin
to describe the visual and tactile richness of colour and
texture of the velvet, raffia and feather trim or the fabrics
that are sometimes a patchwork of different luxurious
weaves. Her interest is in 'natural materials, particularly
linen'. By 'developing soft, heavy fabrics and using special
finishes to give them an antique look', she explains, she
'gives them a soul'.

DANIEL J AS I AK

Patching pieces of interesting fabrics together is something that the young French designer has been doing since he was a child helping his mother do embroidery. Despite having a cult following and a smart shop, Jasiak still hand-washes, bleaches, cuts and sews all of his prototypes himself. He adds to his collection of fabrics – he says he never throws anything away – so that each of his pieces is a composition of different textiles. Jasiak loves blue, and it shows in the varying shades both light and dark in artful combinations that transgress patchwork .

'A-poc' stands for 'a piece of cloth' and is one of Issey Miyake's experiments in textile design. Like 'pleats please', it takes a concept of fabric design – here, the cutting and assembling of one piece of cloth made from a single thread – and displays it in variation and as art. The concept has a showroom and workshop in the Marais by designers Erwan and Ronan Bouroullec (see also p. 26), who've created white polystyrene circular display units to cradle coordinating sporty footwear and accessories. Some articles can be tailored to fit.

46 **Christian Louboutin**

29 19, rue Jean-Jacques-Rousseau

The young designer trained under master Roger Vivier but quickly made a name for himself with his outrageous concepts, including heels made of beer cans. Though Louboutin now claims to be toning down his oeuvre, it's hard to imagine that the man who popularized red soles and heels of lucite with flowers or bits of fashionable rubbish trapped inside will ever become pedestrian ... Celebrities from Cher and Madonna to Princess Caroline of Monaco are fans. The shop is like a mini gallery, each shoe lovingly displayed against gilt foil or in a cubby-hole.

30 **Lucien Pellat-Finet**

12 1, rue Montalembert

Designer Christian Biecher (see also p. 154), who is the designer's interior designer of the moment, has worked his bright magic to create an appropriately striking backdrop for Pellat-Finet's famed cashmere creations. A glass front marked by a pink awning and bright-red display-shelves inside announce knitted wonders, T-shirts, pullovers and belted, tunic-length cardigans. The mere luxury of 100% cashmere is not enough for the designer, who adds stripes, patterns and whimsical cut-out motifs to make eye-catching pieces that range from sporty to sophisticated.

retreat

There is something for everyone wishing to escape the boulevards and the bustle of Paris. The cultural treasures and luscious landscape that have been the playgrounds of kings today offer a realm of gentility, rusticity, artistic inspiration and royal splendour. The four getaways below offer four distinctly different experiences that are united by a love of countryside and by the manmade riches that can be reaped from nature.

St-Germain-en-Laye: A Seat of Kings and a Modern Masterpiece

- Villa Savoye, Poissy
- Cazaudehore 'La Forestière', St-Germain-en-Laye

Lying just at the outskirts of Paris's greater metropolitan area are two exquisite and wonderfully contrasting examples of modern design and genteel rusticity. At the end of a 40-minute suburban train ride, in Poissy, is one of the canonical and most famous residential buildings of the 20th century, designed by Le Corbusier and Jeanneret. A few miles away lies the delightful town of St-Germain-en-Laye, the formal seat of royals before Versailles assumed the role.

Designed by 1928, completed in 1931, saved from demolition in 1958 and restored in 1997, the Villa Savoye is the archetypal modern house – 'poetry produced by technology' – whose form and ideals have had an unparalleled influence on architects and designers around the world. Commissioned by Pierre Savoye for his wife and son on a site with views over the surrounding countryside, the house embodies Le Corbusier's development of domestic architecture as a 'machine for living'. With its main living quarters lifted up a level on stilts to provide the best views (and to allow for a 1927 Citroën to turn around), ramps, a roof terrace, the house's 'cubistic' form is a complete history in modern architecture, a glimpse into the mind of a design visionary.

In sharp but pleasing contrast to the whiteness and pure form of Villa Savoye are the 17th-century stone mansions that give nearby St-Germain-en-Laye, birthplace of Louis XIV, its distinctly patrician air. Soaking up the atmosphere of the town might be enough for some, but for those wanting musical inspiration there is the Musée Claude Debussy, located in the house where the Impressionist composer was born. For sweeping views over the Seine valley and gardens there is the château and its *terrasse*, designed by André le Nôtre (see also p. 180).

Towards the edge of town, on the rim of the St-Germain forest, lies an idyllic inn, 'La Forestière', set amid rose gardens and groves of trees and run since 1928 by generations of the Cazaudehore family, currently Philippe and his wife. While enjoying one of the suitably floral guest rooms or inventive rustic-inspired dishes offered in the acclaimed restaurant, visitors can ponder the richness – and rich contrasts – of French architecture and countryside.

Barbizon: The Nature of Art and Landscape
• Hôtellerie du Bas-Bréau

Barbizon has been known as a 'painters' village' since the early 19th century, when a few landscape painters settled here to take advantage of the inspiration of the enchanting Forest of Fontainebleau. Monet, Pissarro and Camille Corot are known to have painted here, Corot having 'discovered' Barbizon in the 1820s. By mid-century, members of the Barbizon School, naturalist precursors to the Impressionists, had settled in, and the serene little village became a magnet for artists. Today, the tiny hamlet is full of galleries, artists' memorabilia and a number of aesthetically inclined visitors who come to enjoy the lush countryside or to wander down the art-filled rue Grande. The maison-atelier of Jean-François Millet, who became famous for his honest depictions of peasants in rural scenes, and that of Théodore Rousseau are open to the public, as is the Musée Auberge du Père Ganne, a former inn whose walls and furniture are still marked by its artistic clientele.

With an afternoon's fill of the artist colony life, head happily inspired for the distinctly unpeasant-like comforts of the Hôtellerie du Bas-Bréau, a small luxury hotel with spacious rooms, a gourmet restaurant and outdoor swimming pool. You can enjoy a pre-dinner stroll through the park and gardens, perhaps a swim and then settle in for an elegant meal prepared by staff who have entertained ambassadors and royalty. Some rooms include terraces overlooking the forest, a picturesque spot for the hotel's lavish breakfast of fresh fruits, pastries, ham, eggs, juice and coffee. All to keep you fortified for a hike into the 25,000 hectares of forest, where you might encounter the distinctly modern intervention of the *Cyclope*, a typically whimsical metal, mirror and hinged contraption designed by Jean Tinguely and his wife, Nikki de Saint Phalle.

You'll certainly want to save some time and energy for a trip to the grand château and gardens of Vaux le Vicomte, one of Europe's finest formal gardens and a short distance away. Built in 1661 with the finest and most extensive garden created by master landscape designer André Le Nôtre, it was also the inspiration for the envious Louis XIV to create his own grand dwelling – Versailles.

Reims: Champagne Civilization
- Château 'Les Crayères' Gérard Boyer

Reims, a hour and a half by train from Gare de l'Est, is the capital of Champagne, a centre of Gothic splendour and host to one of the finest château-hotels in Europe, if not the world. From the soaring glories of the 13th-century cathedral, under whose vaults most of France's kings were crowned, to the subterranean treasures of the Champagne region's *grands marcs*, Reims provides a refined and sophisticated retreat for those in search of a healthy dose of French history and its epicurean heights.

Three of the city's architectural splendours – the cathedral, the 17th-century Tau palace and the Norman and Gothic Saint Remi abbey and basilica – have been designated UNESCO World Heritage sites for their outstanding beauty. The cathedral's fine Gothic architecture and exceptional collection of stone statues are given a 20th-century twist in the form of stained-glass windows by Marc Chagall, and while the historic buildings might provide the focal points for a cultural visit, Reims is also dotted with numerous examples of Art Déco, the result of a massive post-war reconstruction involving more than 400 architects that took place during the 1920s.

The elegant architecture provides the perfect backdrop to the culture of Champagne, which suffuses many aspects of the otherwise somewhat provincial town. While several of the major Champagne houses offer free tours (G.H. Mumm & Cie, Pommery, Taittinger), a number require prior arrangement – an effort worth making to gain a more intimate understanding of the Champagne arts. Even better, try to arrange a trip into the countryside, where numerous smaller, often family-run producers provide a more personal look at the process, craft and love of making bubbly.

Perhaps Reims's crowning achievement, the stylish blend of culture and gastronomic refinement, is Boyer 'Les Crayères', a distinguished *fin-de-siècle* château located a few minutes by taxi from the historic centre. Set in seven-hectare grounds is one of Europe's finest hotels, run by Elyane and Gérard Boyer, whose three-Michelin-starred cuisine and 19-room accommodation attract a locally discerning clientele and international acclaim.

Le Château d'Esclimont: Palatial Escape
St Symphorien le Château

Located between the magnet attractions of grandeur both secular and sacred, Versailles and Chartres, and only 45 minutes by train from central Paris lies an outstanding French Renaissance château, surrounding by a moat and 150 acres (60 hectares) of parkland that offers fortunate visitors the chance to experience the atmosphere and drama of 16th-century French noble life – with all the modern conveniences. Begun in 1543, the château passed by sale and family through generations of private ownership until it landed in the hands of the Rochefoucauld family who finally sold it to the Grandes Etapes Françaises in 1981. It was turned into an appropriately grand 44-room hotel with decorative and artistic flourishes that preserve the character of a magnificent historic residence.

While some might find the presence of a swimming pool next to a rustic, centuries-old outbuilding disconcerting, others will appreciate the chance to enjoy a swim or a poolside cocktail with a view of the manicured formal gardens. The interiors are a delightful assemblage of period furnishings, wall coverings, painted panellings, gilded woodwork and portraiture. Rooms are a riot of printed fabrics and walls, beds draped and windows looking on to the vast arrangement of parterres, topiary and other plantings. A supremely romantic spot, especially in the evenings when the lit château glitters over the lake. The formal, 18th-century-style restaurant La Rochefoucauld is presided over by chef Olivier Dupart (formerly of Lucas-Carton, p. 140), whose modern menu pays homage to traditional cuisine and local produce. It's fine dining in an incomparable atmosphere. If you need an activity other than wafting about the rooms or exploring the gardens, golf and horse-riding are both on offer or you can visit one of many nearby châteaux or indeed the Gothic glories of magnificent Chartres, just over 16 kilometres (10 miles) away.

contact

All telephone numbers are given for dialling locally: the country code for France is 33; the city code for Paris is 01, which must be dialled before all eight-digit numbers. Calling from abroad, one dials (+33 1) plus the number given below. Telephone numbers in the retreat section are given for dialling from Paris; if calling from abroad, dial the country code (33) and drop the 0 in the number. The number in brackets by the name is the page number on which the entry appears.

Alain Ducasse au Plaza-Athénée [145]
Hôtel Plaza-Athénée
25, avenue Montaigne
75008 Paris
T   01 53 67 65 00
F   53 67 65 12
E   adpa@alain-ducasse.com
W   www.alain-ducasse.com

Alain Mikli [33]
74, rue des Saints-Pères
75007 Paris
T   53 63 87 40
F   56 63 87 49
W   www.mikli.fr

Alexandre Biaggi [163]
14, rue de Seine
75006 Paris
T   44 07 34 73
F   44 07 34 52
E   abiaggi@club-internet.fr

Amaya Eguizabal [68]
45, rue Lépic
75018 Paris
T/F 01 44 92 91 46
E   amayaeguizabal@yahoo.fr

L'Ambroisie [138]
9, place des Vosges
75004 Paris
T   42 78 51 45

Anne Willi [106]
13, rue Keller
75011 Paris
T   01 48 06 74 06
F   48 06 74 04

Antoine et Lili [92]
95, quai de Valmy
75010 Paris
T   40 37 34 86
W   www.antoineetlili.com

L'Apparement [86]
18, rue des Coutures-St-Gervais
75003 Paris
T   48 87 12 22

A-poc [174]
47, rue des Franc-Bourgeois
75004 Paris
T   44 54 07 05
E   a-poc@issey-europe.com
W   www.isseymiyake.com

A Priori Thé [49]
35–37, Galerie Vivienne
75002 Paris
T   42 97 48 75

Les Archives de la Presse [88]
51, rue des Archives
75003 Paris
T   42 72 63 93
F   42 72 93 73

L'Arpège [144]
84, rue de Varenne
75007 Paris
T   47 05 09 06
F   44 18 98 39
E   arpege@alain-passard.com
W   www.alain-passard.com

Artazart [91]
83, quai de Valmy
75010 Paris
T   40 40 24 00
E   info@atrazart.com
W   www.artazart.com

As'Art [54]
3, passage du Grand Cerf
75002 Paris
T   44 88 90 40
F   44 88 90 41

Astier [110]
44, rue Jean-Pierre-Timbaud
75011 Paris
T   43 57 16 35

L'Astrance [139]
4, rue Beethoven
75016 Paris
T   40 50 84 40
F   40 50 11 45

Atelier Renault [41]
53, avenue des Champs-Élysées
75008 Paris
T   49 53 70 70

F   49 53 70 71
W   www.atelier-renault.com

l'Atmosphere [94]
49, rue Lucien-Sampaix
75010 Paris
T   40 38 09 21

Au Bon Marché [166]
24, rue de Sèvres
75007 Paris
T   44 39 80 00
F   44 39 80 50
W   www.lebonmarche.fr

Au Coin de la Rue [43]
10, rue de Castellane
75008 Paris
T   44 71 06 12

L'Avant-Goût [26]
26, rue Bobillot
75013 Paris
T   53 80 24 00

Azzedine Alaïa [81]
7, rue de Moussy
75004 Paris
T   42 72 19 19

Baccarat/Musée du Cristal [95]
30 bis, rue de Paradis
75010 Paris
T   47 70 64 30
W   www.baccarat.fr

Les Bains des Marais [82]
31–33, rue des Blancs-Manteaux
75004 Paris
T   44 61 02 02
F   44 61 02 29
E   contact@
    lesbainsdumarais.com
W www.lesbainsdumarais.com

Le Bamboche (Claude Colliot) [33]
15, rue de Babylone
75007 Paris T 45 49 14 40
F   45 49 14 44

Le Baratin [153]
3, rue Jouye-Rouve
75020 Paris
T   43 49 39 70

La Belle Hortense [87]
31, rue Vieille-du-Temple
75004 Paris
T   48 04 71 60
E   info@cafeine.com
W www.cafeine.com

Belle de Jour [164]
7, rue Tardieu
75018 Paris
T   46 06 15 28
F   42 54 19 47
E   artcristal@yahoo.com

Bercy Village [100]
end of Parc de Bercy
75012 Paris
W www.bercyvillage.com

Bistrot Paul Bert [105]
18, rue Paul-Bert
75011 Paris
T   43 72 24 01

Bistrot Rital [110]
1, rue des Envierges
75020 Paris
T   47 97 08 40

Bô [81]
8, rue St-Merri
75004 Paris
T   42 72 84 64
F   42 72 85 65

Bon [36]
25, rue de la Pompe
75016 Paris
T   40 72 70 00

Le Bourguignon du Marais [83]
52, rue François-Miron
75004 Paris
T   48 87 15 40
F   48 87 17 49

Café Beaubourg [82]
43, rue St-Merri
75004 Paris
T   48 87 63 96

Le Café des Délices [146]
87, rue d'Assas
75006 Paris
T   43 54 70 00
F   43 26 42 05

Café de l'Industrie [108]
16 rue St-Sabin
75011 Paris
T   47 00 13 53

Café Marly [151]
93, rue du Rivoli
75001 Paris
T   49 26 06 60

Café de la Nouvelle Mairie [18]
19–21, rue des Fossés-St-Jacques
75005 Paris
T   44 07 04 41

Café du Passage [106]
12, rue de Charonne
75011 Paris
T   49 29 97 64

Café du Trésor [84]
7–9, rue du Trésor
75004 Paris
T   42 71 78 34

Les Cailloux [26]
58, rue des Cinq-Diamants
75013 Paris
T   45 80 15 08

La Cantine du Faubourg [157]
105, rue du Faubourg-St-Honoré
75008 Paris
T   42 56 22 22

Carré Rive Gauche [35]
E   crg@carrerivegauche.com
W www.carrerivegauche.com

Castelbajac [51]
31, place du Marché-St-Honoré
75001 Paris
T   42 60 41 55

Les Caves Pétrissans [43]
30 bis, avenue Niel
75017 Paris
T   42 27 52 03

Centre Pompidou [81]
place George Pompidou
75004 Paris
T   44 78 12 33
W www.cnac-gp.fr

Chai 33 [100]
33, cour St-Émilion
75012 Paris
T   53 44 01 01
F   53 44 01 02
W www.chai33.com

Les Charpentiers [20]
10, rue Mabillon

75006 Paris
T   43 26 30 05

Chartier [66]
7, rue du Faubourg-Montmartre
Paris 75009
T   47 70 86 29
F   48 24 14 68

Charvet [49]
28, place Vendôme
75001 Paris
T   42 60 30 70

Chez Camille [74]
8, rue Ravignan
75018 Paris
T   46 06 05 78

Chez Casimir [95]
6, rue de Belzunce
75010 Paris
T   48 78 28 80

Chez Georges [135]
1, rue du Mail
75002 Paris
T   42 60 07 11

Chez Paul [26]
22, rue de la Butte-aux-Cailles
75013 Paris
T   45 89 22 11

Chez Prune [92]
71, quai de Valmy
75010 Paris
T   42 41 3047

Chez Ramulaud [106]
269, rue du Faubourg-St-Antoine
75011 Paris
T   43 72 23 29

Le China Club [158]
50, rue de Charenton
75012 Paris
T   43 43 82 02

Christian Astuguevieille [49]
42, Galerie Vivienne
75002 Paris
T   42 60 10 70

Christian Liaigre [33]
42, rue du Bac
75007 Paris
T   53 63 33 66
F   53 63 33 63
E   sales@christian-liaigre.fr

Christian Louboutin [175]
19, rue Jean-Jacques-Rousseau
75001 Paris
T   42 36 05 31
F   42 36 08 56

Christian Tortu [167]
17, rue des Quatre-Vents
75006 Paris
T   56 81 00 24
F   43 25 41 64

Christophe Delcourt [88]
125, rue Vieille-du-Temple
75003 Paris
T   42 78 44 97
F   42 78 79 12

Claude Jeantet [49]
10, rue Therèse
75001 Paris
T/F 42 86 01 36

La Cloche des Halles [53]
28, rue Coquillière
75001 Paris
T   42 36 93 89

Cloître des Billettes [84]
24 rue des Archives
75004 Paris

CMO [49]
5, rue Chabanais
75002 Paris
T   40 20 45 98

Coude Fou [122]
12, rue du Bourg-Tibourg
75004 Paris
T   42 77 15 16

Cojean [64]
4, rue de Sèze
75009 Paris
T   40 06 08 80

Colette [50]
213, rue St-Honoré
75001 Paris
T   55 35 33 90
F   55 35 33 99
E   contact@colette.fr
W www.colette.fr

Comme des Garçons Parfums [164]
23, place du Marché-St-Honoré
75001 Paris
T   47 03 15 03

Comptoir de l'Image [88]
44, rue de Sévigné
75003 Paris
T   42 72 03 92
F   42 72 15 19

La Corbeille [54]
5, passage du Grand-Cerf
75002 Paris
T   53 40 78 77

Les Coteaux [153]
26, boulevard Garibaldi
75015 Paris
T   47 34 83 48

Courrèges [40]
40, rue François 1er
75008 Paris
T   53 67 30 00
F   45 49 23 66

Creations Cherif [103]
13, avenue Daumesnil

75012 Paris
T 43 40 01 00
F 43 40 92 96

Cyrille Varet [103]
67, avenue Daumesnil
75012 Paris
T 44 75 88 88
F 44 75 88 89
E mail@cyrillevaret.com
W www.cyrillevaret.com

Daniel Jasiak [174]
6, rue Cassette
75006 Paris
T 42 22 58 50
F 45 49 23 66

David Emery Creation [71]
52, rue d'Orsel
75018 Paris
T 55 79 76 56
F 42 51 66 30
E contact@davidemerycreation.com
W www.davidemerycreation.com

**Declercq
Passementiers** [57]
15, rue Étienne-Marcel
75001 Paris
T 44 76 90 70
W www.declercqpassementiers.fr

Detaille [66]
10, rue St-Lazare
75009 Paris
T 48 78 68 50
F 40 16 97 18
W www.detaille.com

Le Divan du Monde [67]
75, rue des Martyrs
75018 Paris
T 44 92 77 66
W www.chez.com/naja/divan

Doly'doll [74]
41, rue des Abbesses
75018 Paris
T 42 64 50 11
F 46 06 78 81

Le Dôme [25]
108, boulevard du Montparnasse
75014 Paris
T 43 35 25 81

Le Domicile [81]
25, rue du Renard
75004 Paris
T 44 54 35 36
F 44 54 35 37
E info@ledomicile.fr

Dominique Kieffer [173]
8, rue Hérold
75001 Paris
T 42 21 32 44
F 42 21 31 90
E info@dkieffer.com
W www.dominiquekieffer.com

**Dominique Picquier
Paris** [172]
10, rue Charlot
75003 Paris
T 42 72 39 14
E dominiquepicquier@wanadoo.fr

Doudingue [74]
24, rue Durantin
75018 Paris
T 42 54 88 08

L'Ebauchoir [104]
43–45, rue de Cîteaux
75012 Paris
T 43 42 49 31

L'Ecailler du Bistrot [105]
22, rue Paul-Bert
75011 Paris
T 43 72 76 77

**Editions de Parfums
Frédéric Malle** [165]
37, rue de Grenelle
75007 Paris
T 42 22 77 22
F 42 22 77 33
W www.editionsdeparfums.com

Eglise-du-Dôme [35]
Hôtel des Invalides
75002 Paris
T 44 42 37 72

**Eglise Saint-Jean-de-
Montmartre** [68]
19, rue des Abbesses
75018 Paris
T 46 06 43 96

Le 18 [106]
18, rue Keller
75011 Paris
T 43 38 81 16

Emmanuelle Zysman [68]
81, rue des Martyrs
75018 Paris
T 42 52 01 00
F 42 52 37 27

L'Épi Dupin [33]
11, rue Dupin
75006 Paris
T 42 22 64 56

Epoca [35]
60, rue de Verneuil
75007 Paris
T 45 48 48 66
F 45 44 85 82
E einstein@epoca.fr

Erbalunga [71]
47 bis, rue d'Orsel
75018 Paris
T 42 23 90 21

Et Puis c'est Tout [66]
72, rue des Martyrs
75009 Paris
T 40 23 94 02

Étienne Marcel [57]
34, rue Étienne-Marcel
75002 Paris
T 45 08 01 03

Faerber [50]
12, rue de Castiglione
75001 Paris
T 44 50 50 44
F 44 50 50 42
E contact@idafaerber.com

Fanche et Flo [72]
19, rue Durantin
75018 Paris
T 42 51 24 18
F 42 51 11 39

Fish/La Boissonerie [20]
69, rue de Seine
75006 Paris
T 43 54 34 69

La Flèche d'Or [109]
102 bis, rue de Bagnolet
75020 Paris
T 43 72 04 23
W www.flechedor.com

Florence Dufieux [87]
33, rue de Poitou
75003 Paris
T 42 72 87 79

Florences Loewy [86]
9–11, rue de Thorigny
75003 Paris
T 44 78 98 45
F 44 78 98 46
E flo@florenceloewy.com
W www.florenceloewy.com

La Folie en Tête [26]
33, rue de la Butte-aux-Cailles
75013 Paris
T 45 80 65 99

Fondation Cartier [25]
261, boulevard Raspail
75014 Paris
T 42 18 56 51
F 42 18 56 52
W www.fondation.cartier.fr

Fondation Le Corbusier [38]
8–10, square du Docteur-Blanche
75016 Paris
T 42 88 41 53
F 42 88 33 17
W www.fondationlecorbusier.
asso.fr

**Fondation Dina Vierny –
Musée Maillol** [35]
59–61, rue de Grenelle
75007 Paris
T 42 22 59 58
F 42 84 14 02
E contact@museemaillol.com
W www.museemaillol.com

Fondation Icar [92]
159, quai de Valmy

75010 Paris
T 53 26 36 61
E info@icarfoundation.org
W www.icarfoundation.org

Les Fontaines [17]
9, rue Soufflot
75005 Paris
T 43 26 42 80

La Fourmi [68]
74 rue des Martyrs
75018 Paris
T 42 64 74 28

Le Fumoir [52]
6, rue de l'Amiral-de-Coligny
75001 Paris
T 42 92 00 24

**FuturWare/Tatiana Lebedev
Boutique** [72]
2, rue Piémontési
75018 Paris
T 42 23 66 08
F 42 23 66 09

Gaëlle Barré [106]
17, rue Keller
75011 Paris
T 43 14 63 02
F 43 14 63 09

Galerie 54 [22]
54, rue Mazarine
75006 Paris
T 43 26 89 96

**La Galerie
d'Architecture** [81]
11, rue des Blancs-Manteaux
75004 Paris
T 49 96 64 00
F 49 96 64 01
E mail@galerie-architecture.fr
W www.galerie-architecture.fr

Galerie Chez Valentin [88]
9, rue St-Gilles
75003 Paris
T 48 87 42 55

**Galerie Christine
Diegoni** [71]
47ter, rue d'Orsel
75018 Paris
T 42 64 69 48
F 42 58 21 64

Galerie Hélène Porée [20]
1, rue de l'Odeon
75006 Paris
T 43 54 17 00
F 43 54 17 02
W www.galerie-helene-poree.fr

Galerie du Passage [53]
20, passage Véro-Dodat
75001 Paris
T 42 36 01 13
F 40 41 98 86

Galerie Patrick Seguin [162]
34, rue de Charonne
75011 Paris
T   47 00 32 35

Galerie Pierre [88]
22, rue Debelleyme
75003 Paris
T   42 72 20 24
F   42 72 20 29
E   galeriepierre@aol.com

Galerie Vivienne [49]
off rue des Petits-Champs
75001 Paris

Galerie Yves Gastou [162]
12, rue Bonaparte
75006 Paris
T   53 73 00 10
F   53 73 00 12
E   galeriegastou@noos.fr
W   www.galerieyvesgastou.com

Gallopin [137]
40, rue Notre-Dame-des-Victoires
75002 Paris
T   42 36 45 38

Gaspard de la Butte [73]
10 bis, rue Yvonne-Le-Tac
75018 Paris
T   42 55 99 40

Georges [81]
6th Floor
Centre Pompidou
75004 Paris
T   44 78 47 99

Gilles Oudin [68]
20, avenue de Trudaine
75009 Paris
T/F 48 74 04 24
E   gillesoudin@libertysurf.fr

Ginette de la Côte d'Azur [74]
101, rue Caulaincourt
75018 Paris
T   46 06 01 49

Le Grand Véfour [136]
17, rue de Beaujolais
75001 Paris
T   42 96 56 27

Guy Savoy [134]
18, rue Troyon
75017 Paris
T   43 80 40 61
F   46 22 43 09
W   www.guysavoy.com

L'Habilleur [86]
44, rue de Poitou
75003 Paris
T   48 87 77 12

Heaven [68]
83, rue des Martyrs
75018 Paris

T   44 92 92 92
W   www.heaven-paris.com

L'Hotel [126]
13, rue des Beaux-Arts
75006 Paris
T   44 41 99 00
F   43 25 64 81
E   reservation@l-hotel.com
W   www.l-hotel.com

Hôtel Costes [159]
239, rue St-Honoré
75001 Paris
T   42 44 50 00
F   42 44 50 01

Hôtel du Bourg Tibourg [122]
19, rue du Bourg-Tibourg
75004 Paris
T   42 78 47 39
F   40 29 07 00
E   hotel.du.bourg.tibourg@
wanadoo.fr

Hôtel Duc de Saint-Simon [130]
14, rue de St-Simon
75007 Paris
T   44 39 20 20
F   45 48 68 25
E   duc.de.saint.simon@
wanadoo.fr

Hotel des Grandes Ecole [120]
75, rue du Cardinal-Lemoine
75005 Paris
T   43 26 79 23
F   43 25 28 15
E   hotel.grandes.ecoles
@wanadoo.fr
W   www.hotel-grandes-
ecoles.com

Hotel Square [118]
3, rue de Boulainvilliers
75016 Paris
T   44 14 91 90
F   44 14 91 99
E   hotel.square@wandadoo.fr
W   www.hotelsquare.com

Hôtel de Vendôme [116]
1, place Vendôme
75001 Paris
T   55 04 55 00
F   49 27 97 89
E   reservations@
hoteldevendome.com
W   www.hoteldevendome.com

La Hune [23]
170, boulevard St-Germain
75006 Paris
T   45 48 35 85
F   45 44 49 87

IF [22]
20, rue Jacob
75006 Paris
T   42 34 54 64
F   42 34 54 66

Institute du Monde Arabe [17]
1, rue des Fossés-St-Bernard
75005 Paris
T   40 51 38 38
F   43 54 76 45
W   www.imarabe.org

Isabel Marant [168]
16, rue de Charonne
75011 Paris
T   49 29 71 55

Jacques Le Corre [170]
193, rue St-Honoré
75001 Paris
T   42 96 97 40

Jamin Puech [169]
61, rue d'Hauteville
75010 Paris
T/F 40 22 08 32
W   www.jamin-puech.com

JAR [165]
14, rue de Castiglione
75001 Paris
T   40 20 47 20

Jean-Louis Pinabel [54]
4, passage du Grand Cerf
75002 Paris
T   40 28 41 61
F   40 28 48 66
E   info@jean-louis-pinabel.com
W   www.jean-louis-pinabel.com

Jean Paul Gaultier [43]
44, avenue George V
75008 Paris
T   44 43 00 44

6, Galerie Vivienne [49]
75002 Paris
T   42 86 05 05
W   www.jeanpaulgaultier.com

Jérémie Barthod [71]
7, rue des Trois-Frères
75018 Paris
T   42 62 54 50
F   43 87 58 61

José Levy [87]
70, rue Vieille-du-Temple
75003 Paris
T 01 48 04 39 16

Jules Verne [137]
Eiffel Tower
Champs-de-Mars
75007 Paris
T   45 55 61 44
F   47 05 29 41
W   www.tour-eiffel.fr

Juvenile's [49]
47, rue de Richelieu
75001 Paris
T   42 97 46 49
F   42 60 31 52

Karine Dupont [87]
22, rue de Poitou
75003 Paris
T   40 27 84 94
F   40 27 83 84
W   www.karinedupont.com

Kazana [71]
3, rue Tardieu
75018 Paris
T   42 59 41 02

Killiwatch [54]
64, rue Tiquetonne
75002 Paris
T   42 21 17 37

Kyungmee J. [84]
38, rue du Roi-du-Sicilie
75004 Paris
T   42 74 33 85
E   KyungmeeJ@compuserve.com

Lagerfeld Gallery [25]
40, rue de Seine
75006 Paris
T   55 42 75 51
F   55 42 75 30

Lasserre [147]
17, avenue Franklin-Roosevelt
75008 Paris
T   43 59 02 13
F   45 63 72 23

Le Lèche-Vin [108]
13, rue Daval
75011 Paris
T   43 55 98 91

Legrand Filles et Fils [152]
1, rue de la Banque
75002 Paris
T   42 60 07 12
F   42 61 25 51

Librairie Gourmande [18]
4, rue Dante
75005 Paris
T   43 54 37 27
F   43 54 31 16
W   www.librairie-gourmande.fr

Librairie le Moniteur [18]
7, place de l'Odeon
75006 Paris
T   44 41 15 75
F   40 51 85 98
W   www.groupemoniteur.fr

L'Ile Enchantée [94]
65, boulevard de la Villette
75010 Paris
T   42 01 67 99

Louvre des Antiquaires [51]
2, place du Palais-Royal
75001 Paris
T   42 97 27 00
F   42 97 00 14
W   www.louvre-antiquaires.com

Lucas-Carton [140]
9, place de la Madeleine
75008 Paris
T   42 65 22 90

Lucien Pellat-Finet [175]
1, rue Montalembert
75007 Paris
T   42 22 22 77
F   42 22 77 00

Mairie du 9e [64]
6, rue Drouot
75009 Paris
T   42 46 72 09

La Maison de l'Aubrac [40]
37, rue Marbeuf
75008 Paris
T   43 59 05 14
F   42 89 66 09

La Maison Blanche [43]
15, avenue Montaigne
75008 Paris
T   47 23 55 99

Maison Fey [103]
15, avenue Daumesnil
75012 Paris
T   43 41 22 22
F   43 41 11 12
E   contact@maisonfey.com
W   www.maisonfey.com

**La Maison des Trois
Thés** [150]
33, rue Gracieuse
75005 Paris
T   43 36 93 84

Malhia [103]
19, avenue Daumesnil
75012 Paris
T   53 44 76 76
F   53 44 76 77
W   www.malhia.com

Mandarina Duck [50]
7, boulevard de la Madeleine
75002 Paris
T   42 86 08 00
W   www.mandarinaduck.com

Marché d'Aligre [103]
place d'Aligre
75012 Paris

Marie Lavande [103]
83, avenue Daumesnil
75012 Paris
T   44 67 78 78
F   44 67 01 78
W   www.marie-lavande.com

Marie-Lise Goëlo [54]
10, passage du Grand Cerf
75002 Paris
T   42 36 66 69

La Marine [91]
55 bis, quai de Valmy

75010 Paris
T   42 39 69 81

Market [41]
15, avenue Matignon
75008 Paris
T   56 43 40 90

Mars [88]
15, rue Debelleyme
75003 Paris
T/F 42 71 19 54

Martin Grant [84]
32, rue des Rosiers
75004 Paris
T   42 71 39 49
F   42 71 37 77

La Mère de Famille [67]
35, rue du Faubourg-Montmartre
75009 Paris
T   47 70 83 69

La Mère Lachaise [111]
78, boulevard de Ménilmontant
75020 Paris
T   47 97 61 60

Michèle Bonny [71]
6, place Charles-Dullin
75018 Paris
T   42 52 00 1

La Mosquée de Paris [150]
39, rue Geoffroy-St-Hilaire
75005 Paris
T   43 31 38 20

Le Musée Cognacq-Jay [88]
8, rue Elzévir
75003 Paris
T   40 27 07 21
F   40 27 89 44
W   www.paris-france.org/
musees/cognacq_jay

Musée Gustave Moreau [62]
14, rue de La Rochefoucauld
75009 Paris
T   48 74 38 50

**Musée Jacquemart
André** [62]
158, boulevard Haussmann
75008 Paris
T   45 62 11 59
F   45 62 16 36
W   www.musee-jacquemart-
andre.com

**Musée Nissim de
Camondo** [62]
63, rue de Monceau
75008 Paris
T   53 89 06 40
F   53 89 06 42
W   www.ucad.fr/ucad/musee_
nissim_camodo.html

Musée Rodin [33]
Hôtel Biron
77, rue de Varenne

75007 Paris
T   44 18 61 10
F   44 18 61 30
E   penseur@musee-rodin.fr
W   www.musee-rodin.fr

**Musée de la Vie
Romantique** [64]
Hôtel Scheffer-Renan
16, rue Chaptal
75009 Paris
T   48 74 95 38
F   48 74 28 42

Nirvana [158]
3, avenue Matignon
75008 Paris
T   42 89 64 72

Noir Ebène [108]
9 and 22, rue Oberkampf
75011 Paris
T   43 57 80 50

L'Oeil du Huit [62]
8, rue Milton
75009 Paris
T/F 40 23 02 92
E   oeilduhuit@aol.fr
W   www.artw3.com/oeildu8

Oona L'Ourse [20]
72, rue Madame
75006 Paris
T   42 84 11 94

**Pages 50/70 – Olivier
Verlet** [74]
15, rue Yvonne-Le-Tac
75018 Paris
T   42 52 48 59
E   olivier.verlet@wanadoo.fr

La Pagode [35]
57 bis, rue de Babylone
75007 Paris
T   45 55 48 48

Palais de Tokyo [39]
13, avenue du Président-Wilson
75016 Paris
T   47 23 54 01

La Palette [23]
43, rue de Seine
75006 Paris
T   43 26 68 15

Papier+ [84]
9, rue du Pont Louis-Philippe
75004 Paris
T   42 77 70 49
F   48 87 37 60
E   papier.plus@wanadoo.fr
W   www.papierplus.com

Parc André Citroën [36]
Via quai André-Citroën
75015 Paris

Passage [87]
41, rue de Poitou
75003 Paris

Passage d'Enfer [25]
off boulevard Raspail
75014 Paris

Passage de Retz [154]
9, rue Charlot
75003 Paris
T   48 04 37 99
F   48 04 38 60

Passage du Grand Cerf [54]
between rue St-Dennis and
rue Dussoubs
75002 Paris

Passiflore [38]
33, rue de Longchamp
75116 Paris
T   47 04 96 81
F   47 04 32 27

Patricia Louisor [73]
16, rue Houdon
75018 Paris
T   42 62 10 42
F   42 62 35 03

Patrick Fourtin [52]
9, rue des Bons-Enfants
75001 Paris
T   42 60 12 63
F   42 60 19 63
W   www.antikaparis.com/fourtin

Pause Café [106]
41, rue de Charonne
75011 Paris
T   48 06 80 33

**Le Pavillon de
l'Arsenal** [103]
21, boulevard Morland
75004 Paris
T   42 76 33 97
F   42 76 26 32
E   inpa@pavillon-arsenal.com
W   www.pavillon-arsenal.com

Pavillon de Paris [128]
7, rue de Parme
75009 Paris
T   55 31 60 00
F   55 31 60 01
E   mail@pavillondeparis.com
W   www.pavillondeparis.com

Peggy Huyn Kinh [171]
11, rue Coëtlogon
75006 Paris
T   42 84 83 83
F   42 84 83 84
E   info@phk.fr
W   www.peggy-huyn-kinh.fr

Pershing Hall [124]
49, rue Pierre-Charron
75008 Paris
T   58 36 58 00
F   58 36 58 01
E   info@pershinghall.com
W   www.pershing-hall.com

Le Petit Pontoise [17]
9, rue de Pontoise
75005 Paris
T 43 29 25 20

Petrossian [143]
18, boulevard de La Tour-
Maubourg
75007 Paris
T 44 11 32 32

Philippe Modal [51]
33, place du Marché-St-Honoré
75001 Paris
T 42 96 89 02

Pierre Gagnaire [142]
Hotel Balzac
6, rue Balzac
75008 Paris
T 58 36 12 50

Pierre Hermé [167]
72, rue Bonaparte
75006 Paris
T 43 54 47 77

Plaza Athenée [155]
25, avenue Montaigne
75008 Paris
T 53 67 65 00

PM & Co. [54]
5, passage du Grand Cerf
75002 Paris
T 55 80 71 06

Le Pré Catalan [141]
route de Suresnes
Bois de Boulogne
75016 Paris
T 44 14 41 14

**Les Puces de Saint-
Ouen** [74]
avenue de St-Ouen
75017 Paris

La Régalade [143]
49, avenue Jean-Moulin
75014 Paris
T 45 45 68 58

R'aliment [88]
57, rue Charlot
75003 Paris
T 48 04 88 28
F 48 04 88 28
E contact@r-aliment.com
W www.resodesign.com

Resodiversion [88]
43, rue Charlot
75003 Paris
T 44 59 32 16
F 53 01 99 14
W www.resodesign.com

Résonances [100]
Bercy-Village
9, Cour St-Émilion
75012 Paris
T 44 73 82 82

F 44 73 82 83
E bercy.village@resonances.fr
W www.resonances.fr

Rodolphe Ménudier [171]
14, rue Castiglione
75001 Paris
T 42 60 86 27

Rosebud [25]
11 bis, rue Delambre
75014 Paris
T 43 35 38 54

Sandrine Philippe [54]
6, rue Hérold
75001 Paris
T 40 26 21 78
F 48 87 62 53

Sentou Galerie [163]
18 and 24, rue du Pont Louis-
Philippe
75004 Paris
T 42 77 44 79
F 48 87 67 14
29, rue François-Miron
Paris 75004
T 42 78 50 60
F 42 78 55 66
E sentoumarais@sentou.fr
26, boulevard Raspail
75007 Paris
T 45 49 00 05
F 45 49 98 05
E sentouraspail@sentou.fr
W www.sentou.fr

Serge Amoruso [83]
39, rue du Roi-de-Sicile
75004 Paris
T 48 04 97 97
F 42 76 90 33
E info@sergeamorusoparis.com
W www.sergeamorusoparis.com

6 New York [38]
6, avenue de New-York
75116 Paris
T 40 70 03 30

Le Soleil [74]
109, avenue Michelet
75018 Paris
T 40 10 08 08

Le Souk [106]
1, rue Keller
75011 Paris
T 49 29 05 08

Spoon, Food & Wine [138]
12, rue de Marignan
75008 Paris
T 40 76 34 44

Le Square Trousseau [104]
1, rue Antoine-Vollon
75012 Paris
T 43 43 06 00
F 43 43 00 66

Stella Cadente [91]
93, quai de Valmy
Paris 75010
T 42 09 27 00

Theatre de l'Atelier [71]
1, place Charles-Dullin
75018 Paris
T 46 06 49 24
W www.theatre-atelier.com

Le Train Bleu [103]
Gare de Lyon
place Louis Armand
75012 Paris
T 43 43 09 06

Vanessa Bruno [20]
25, rue St-Sulpice
75006 Paris
T 43 54 41 04

Velly [67]
52, rue Lamartine
75009 Paris
T 48 78 60 05

Le Verre Volé [152]
67, rue de Lancry
75010 Paris
T 48 03 17 34

Vertical [103]
63, avenue Daumesnil
75012 Paris
T 43 40 26 26
F 43 40 34 34
E courrier@vertical.fr
W perso.club-internet.fr/lanore/

**VIA (Valorisation de
l'Innovations dans
l'Ameublement)** [103]
29–33, avenue Daumesnil
75012 Paris
T 46 28 11 11
F 46 28 13 13
E via@mobilier.com
W www.via.asso.fr

Viaduc des Arts [103]
1-129, avenue Daumesnil
75012 Paris
E assovda@viaduc-des-arts.com
W www.viaduc-des-arts.com

Le Viaduc Café [103]
43, avenue Daumesnil
75012 Paris
T 44 74 70 70
F 44 74 70 71

Le Villaret [142]
13, rue Ternaux
75011 Paris
T 43 57 89 76

Le Vin des Rues [26]
21, rue Boulard
75014 Paris
T 43 22 19 78

Le Vin de Zinc [109]
25, rue Oberkampf
75011 Paris
T 48 06 28 23

Le Wax [156]
15, rue Daval
75011 Paris
T 40 21 16 16

Ze Kitchen Galerie [144]
4, rue des Grands-Augustins
75006 Paris
T 44 32 00 32
F 44 32 00 33
E zekitchen.galerie@wanadoo.fr

**Zelia sur la Terre comme au
Ciel** [71]
47ter, rue d'Orsel
75018 Paris
T 46 06 96 51
E zelia@zelia.net
W www.zelia.net

Le Zéphyr [111]
1, rue du Jourdain
75020 Paris
T 46 36 65 81

SAINT-GERMAIN-EN-LAYE [178]
*Take the RER A1, a commuter line
leaving from a number of central
Paris Métro stops, to Saint-
Germain-en-Laye, about a 40-
minute journey. Villa Savoye is
located in Poissy, about a 10-
minute taxi ride (costing €15) from
the hotel. Alternatively, take the
RER A5 from a central Paris Métro
stop to Poissy for the Villa Savoye,
and take a taxi from there to the
hotel.*

Villa Savoye
82, rue de Villiers
78300 Poissy
T   39 65 01 06
F   39 65 19 33
E   villa-savoye@monuments-
       france.fr
Open every day except Tuesdays
(call to confirm opening times)

Cazaudehore et 'La Forestière'
Hotel
1, avenue Kennedy
78100 St-Germain-en-Laye
T   30 61 64 64
F   39 73 73 88
E   cazaudehore@
       relaischateaux.com
W   www.cazaudehore.fr
Double rooms from €190

BARBIZON [180]
*Barbizon is most easily reached by
taking a 40-minute train ride, which
leaves from Gare de Lyon, to
Fontainebleau. From there, it is
approximately a 15-minute taxi ride
(costing about €20) to Barbizon and
the hotel.*

Hôtellerie du Bas-Bréau
22, Rue Grande
77630 Barbizon
T   60 66 40 05
F   60 69 22 89
W   basbreau@wanadoo.fr
E   www.bas-breau.com
Double rooms from €250

Vaux le Vicomte
77950 Maincy
T   64 14 41 90
F   60.69.90.85
W   www.vaux-le-vicomte.com

REIMS [182]
*Reims is approximately a 90-minute
train journey from Paris's Gare
d'Est; trains leave about every hour.
The hotel is located about ten
minutes from the city centre by taxi
(approximately €10).*

Château 'Les Crayères' Gérard
Boyer
64, boulevard Henry Vasnier
51100 Reims
T   03 26 82 80 80
F   03 26 82 65 52
E   crayeres@gerardboyer.com
W   www.gerardboyer.com
Double rooms from €350

CHÂTEAU D'ESCLIMONT [184]
*Take the 35- to 50-minute train
journey from Gare Montparnasse to
Rambouillet. From there the
château is about a 20-minute taxi
journey (costing €25 to 30).*

Chateau d'Esclimont
28700 St Symphorien le Château
T   02 37 31 15 15
F   02 37 31 57 91
E   contact@esclimont.com
W   www.esclimont.com
Double rooms from €250